SHARPENING

SMALL TOOLS

AND SOME DOMESTIC APPLIANCES

Ian Bradley

Completely revised edition

Model & Allied Publications

Model and Allied Publications
Argus Books Ltd.
P.O. Box 35
Hemel Hempstead
Herts, England.

ST/22/KK.

First Published 1948
Second Impression 1951
Third Impression 1955
Fourth Impression 1963
Fifth Impression 1968
Sixth Impression 1971
Seventh Impression 1972
Eighth Impression 1974
New revised edition 1976
Tenth Impression 1979
Eleventh Impression 1982

© Model and Allied Publications Ltd. 1948

© Argus Books Ltd. and Ian Bradley 1976

ISBN 0 85242 459 0

Printed by A. Wheaton & Co. Ltd., Exeter

PREFACE

IF it be allowed that sharp tools are essential for good work, then there is little need for excuse in offering a small book on this important subject to those interested in metalworking or carpentry ; whilst, as a topic of, perhaps, more general interest, a short account is included of sharpening some common domestic appliances.

In the following pages the sharpening of tools in general use only is dealt with, and, whenever possible, simple and well-tried methods have been adopted, bearing in mind that usually the aim when sharpening a tool should be to restore, as accurately and as consistently as possible, the original form of its cutting edge.

This new edition has been considerably revised to include eight new pages of illustrations and notes which amplify some of the methods and techniques described in the text. Some of the original illustrations have also been replaced.

CONTENTS

CHAPTER I

SHARPENING MATERIALS

SINCE the earliest times, the abrasive properties of natural stones and rocks have been utilised for sharpening metal tools and weapons. These natural deposits vary from the hard, close-grained quartz rocks to the softer and more friable sand stones.

Anyone who has tried to sharpen a pocket knife on a doorstep will have discovered that, when the stone is used dry, it will soon become filled with metal particles, and in that state it will have but little abrasive action. To obviate this, water or oil is applied to the stone to enable the metal dust to be carried away and prevent its becoming adherent to the surface of the stone.

Whether water or oil should be used will depend on the character of the stone employed. In general, the thinner the oil or other liquid used the faster the stone will cut, for the presence of the oil has a cushioning effect on the cutting properties of the stone, in addition to preventing the adherence of metallic dust.

THE ARKANSAS STONE. This is, perhaps, the best known form of oilstone and the most generally used. It is found as a natural deposit in the American State of Arkansas, and the best samples consist of nearly pure quartz almost white in colour.

There is no apparent grain in the stone and its extreme hardness prevents the surface from being worn unevenly, and scored or grooved when tools with narrow cutting edges are sharpened on it. The outstanding characteristic of this stone is the facility with which it imparts an extremely accurate and highly finished edge to all classes of cutting tools.

As the Arkansas stone is expensive, especially in the best grades, it should be well cared for and protected from damage by means of a wooden casing fitted with a lid, as illustrated in Fig. 1. To prevent the stone from sliding on the bench when in use, points may be fitted to the sole of the casing, or a cross-piece can be attached to engage the edge of the bench or the lathe bed.

THE WASHITA STONE. Although this oilstone is much cheaper than the foregoing variety, its qualities are greatly inferior. It is comparatively coarse grained, and its softer texture does not well resist wear or scoring when it is used to sharpen pointed or narrow-edged tools.

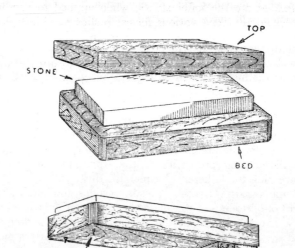

TOP

STONE

BED

FOR THE JOINER
POINTS AT EACH END
ALLOW BED TO GRIP
BENCH FIRMLY

FOR THE TURNER
FILLET AT EACH END
TO FIT TRANSVERSELY
ON LATHE BED

Fig. 1.

TURKEY STONE. The texture of this form of oilstone varies greatly ; the hardest stones are capable of producing a very fine cutting edge, whilst the softer qualities cut more rapidly but are too readily grooved to be suitable for sharpening tools such as gravers and small chisels.

OILSTONE SLIPS. In addition to the ordinary bench forms or blocks, oilstones of all types, but Arkansas stones in particular, are made as slips for holding in the hand and applying to the tool. These slips are made in a great variety of shapes for use when sharpening tools of special form, such as gouges and reamers, but the flat rectangular patterns are suitable for touching-up the cutting edges of lathe and shaper tools while clamped in the toolpost of the machine. Hard Arkansas slips are particularly suited for this purpose, for not only do they produce a very fine cutting edge, but they are not so liable to be scored, as are the softer stones, when applied to narrow cutting edges. The various forms of slips are illustrated later in Fig. 2, in connection with hones composed of artificial abrasive material.

RAZOR HONES. These stones are usually of soft texture, and free-cutting is promoted by using water, instead of oil, as a lubricant. The best known stones come from Germany and Belgium, but the British varieties are now largely used in this country.

Stones of this type are employed almost exclusively for honing razors, where the blade is laid flat to the surface of the stone during the sharpening operation, but if a tool, such as a chisel, is applied to the stone at the usual angle for sharpening, the cutting edge will tend to dig in and plough up the surface.

GRINDSTONES. These circular stones, formed from natural sandstone deposits, were formerly used exclusively in the cutlery industry and may still be found in carpenters' shops.

In order to prevent heating of the work and to promote free-cutting, the stone is kept flooded with water by means of a drip can or by dipping into a self-contained water tank.

As these stones are of soft texture and have a definite grain, they tend to wear irregularly and may require truing from time to time by means of a piece of hoop-iron or with a tool specially designed for the purpose.

ARTIFICIAL ABRASIVES. It will be evident that the abrasive stones, found as natural deposits in many parts

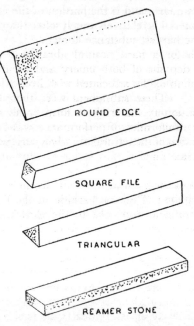

ROUND EDGE

SQUARE FILE

TRIANGULAR

REAMER STONE

Fig. 2.

of the world, have certain disadvantages ; the finished product has to be fashioned from the quarried stone either by grinding or cutting, which is a laborious and expensive process : the material is seldom homogeneous, and may be interspersed with veins of impurities : the nature of the stone may vary in different parts of the same quarry, thus rendering uniformity of output hardly possible.

For these reasons, a natural abrasive material was sought which could be embedded in a bonding substance to afford all the advantages of the natural stone, and, at the same time, ensure uniformity and allow of precise composition capable of being varied to meet special requirements.

As has been stated, the Arkansas stone is composed of nearly pure quartz and is the hardest of the natural hones, but this material is relatively much softer than the diamond which is the hardest substance known.

A search for a hard natural abrasive resulted in the finding of deposits of both emery and corundum, which are aluminium oxides associated with iron-oxide and other impurities. These substances were then bonded with ceramic or pottery materials to form hones and grinding wheels, but uniformity of performance was lacking owing to the variation of the natural abrasives even when quarried from the same mine.

However, research led to the discovery of the artificial production of the natural materials in their pure form.

The formation of Silicon carbide in the laboratory, by the fusion of sand and coke in the electric furnace, was later followed by the production of aluminium oxide abrasives from the aluminium ore bauxite.

Grinding wheels and hones made from either the silicon or the aluminium artificial compounds are superior to those where the natural materials are used, both as regards the uniformity and the quality of the work produced.

The Norton Grinding Wheel Co., who were pioneers in the field of artificially-produced abrasives, have adopted the name Crystolon to indicate the silicon carbide compound, and have designated the factory-produced aluminium oxide, Alundum.

ARTIFICIAL ABRASIVE STONES. Carborundum stones for bench or hand use are made by many of the leading manufacturers of artificial abrasive materials. The hones manufactured by the Norton Grinding Wheel Co., are named India stones, and these are made in the ordinary bench size of 8 in. long, 2 in. wide, and 1 in. thick, and also in the form of slips or hand stones.

All these varieties can be obtained in either fine, medium, or coarse grit-size suitable for fine or rough sharpening respectively.

India stones are very resistant to wear, and their surface hardness protects them against scoring when tools with a narrow or pointed cutting edge are sharpened.

In addition to the size mentioned, the bench stones are made in a variety of sizes and also in the form of combination stones, composed of two portions of different grit-size cemented together. Some of the more generally used forms of slips manufactured are illustrated in Fig. 2 ; and the special use of these will be described in the appropriate place later in this book.

In accordance with the manufacturer's recommendations, adoption of the following measures are essential for the preservation of the cutting efficiency of these stones ; the initial sharpness is preserved by keeping the stone clean and moist, that is to say by wiping after use and applying a little thin oil to prevent hardening of the surface, also when not in use the stone should be kept in its covered box to exclude dust and air. Secondly, the flat surface of the stone should be preserved by careful use, and to prevent uneven wear the whole surface should be employed and not merely the centre portion. As a further precaution, the side-face of the stone should be used if there is any danger of the surface being damaged when sharpening a pointed tool. Glazing and loading should be prevented by regular oiling and cleaning, for the surface oil floats off the metallic dust and prevents its entry into the substance of the stone. Should the stone become glazed or gummed with dried oil, its cutting properties can usually be restored by cleaning the surface with petrol or ammonia ; but if this does not suffice, the stone should be rubbed with a piece of fine sandpaper fixed to a smooth, flat board.

GRINDING WHEELS. Although grinding wheels are now

made by a large number of manufacturers in various parts of the world, fortunately, the terms adopted to designate the character and properties of the wheels are common to all the well-known makes.

As has already been stated, the two artificial abrasives most commonly used are silicon carbide and aluminium oxide, which are manufactured by the Norton Co., as Crystolon and Alundum respectively ; the former is used chiefly for grinding cast-iron and non-ferrous metals, and the latter for tool sharpening and surface grinding.

GRAIN SIZE. It is important that the abrasive grains should be of uniform size, otherwise the small grains will not do their share of the work and any large grains will tend to produce scratch marks and thus spoil the surface finish.

The segregation of the grains according to size is carried out by an accurately controlled sieving operation. The Alundum grain sizes range from 4 to 900 ; that is to say these figures represent the number of meshes per linear inch in the screen through which the abrasive material has passed.

For rough-grinding small tools a grain-size of from 24 to 40 is generally used, whilst for finishing the work a 50 to 80 grit will be found to give good results.

GRADE. The abrasive grains are embedded in a matrix or bonding substance of which there are two forms in general use, the vitrified and the silicate. The former is more generally suitable for the large variety of work undertaken in the small workshop.

The bonding material is graded not according to its hardness, but by the degree of tenacity with which it holds the abrasive grains.

When a grinding wheel is in operation the abrasive grains gradually become blunted, and if the wheel is to continue to cut efficiently and without unduly heating the work, it is important that these blunted grains should be shed so that fresh, sharp grains can take their place.

The **grade**, or tenacity of holding of the bonding material must, therefore, be such that the sharp, free-cutting grains are securely held, whilst the blunted grains are removed by the pressure of the work.

The grade of the wheel is denoted by a letter ; H signifies hard, M medium, and S soft ; likewise, the intermediate grades are represented by the intervening letters of the alphabet.

For general workshop use and rough grinding, a wheel with a vitrified bond of from H to K grade should be used, whilst for fine grinding a softer grade of from J to M will be found suitable.

When sharpening tools such as scribers and very small boring tools, the ordinary wheel used for finish-grinding will probably be found to remove the metal too quickly for the operation to be readily controlled. In this case, the small India wheels made by the Norton Co. will be found to give excellent results, but thin oil should be applied to the wheel-surface to prevent its becoming loaded with metal dust and thus causing heating of the work.

A special green grit type of wheel is necessary for sharpening Tungsten carbide-tipped tools, and, to obtain a really fine cutting edge, this must be followed by lapping on a wheel impregnated with diamond dust.

CARE OF GRINDING WHEELS. If a wheel is to continue to give good service it must be run at the correct speed and be properly cared for. The question of mounting and truing the wheel will be dealt with later when grinding appliances are considered. Normally the wheel should be set to run at some 5,000 ft. per min., measured at the periphery ; or if the revolutions per min. are required, this is ascertained by dividing the number 20,000 by the diameter of the wheel expressed in inches.

The table on page 9 gives the exact calculated speeds.

The two common adverse conditions that may arise to interfere with the effective working of the wheel are **glazing** and **loading**.

WHEEL DIAM. IN INCHES	REVOLUTIONS PER MINUTE FOR SURFACE SPEEDS OF		
	4,000	5,000	6,000
1	15,279	19,099	22,918
2	7,639	9,549	11,459
3	5,093	6,366	7,639
4	3,820	4,775	5,730
5	3,056	3,820	4,584
6	2,546	3,183	3,820
7	2,183	2,728	3,274
8	1,910	2,387	2,865

GLAZING. If the abrasive particles after becoming blunted are not shed from the surface, the wheel will cease to cut efficiently and is said to be glazed ; this causes rubbing, as opposed to cutting, and results in undue heating of the work.

The condition of the wheel can be restored by the application of a wheel dresser to remove the blunt particles and expose fresh cutting grains. Should the trouble tend to recur, the remedy is either to run the wheel at a lower speed, or to substitute a wheel of softer grade, that is to say one with a less tenacious bonding material.

LOADING. This takes place when the surface of the wheel becomes filled with adherent metal particles, as is seen in the case of a clogged file ; the wheel's cutting action then almost ceases, and great heat is produced by the friction of the metal particles rubbing against the work.

This condition arises when the work is forced against the wheel, or if soft material, such as mild steel, is ground on a wheel unsuitable for this purpose.

The cutting properties of the wheel must be restored by using a wheel dresser to remove the damaged surface, and, thereafter, only hardened steel should be ground, and without excessive pressure being applied. In addition, increasing the wheel speed will help to prevent loading.

India wheels can be kept in good cutting condition by observing the recommendations made for the maintenance of bench India stones.

WHEEL DRESSERS. Wheels can be trued and their cutting surface restored by means of a hand-tool in the end of which a diamond is mounted. The shank of the tool should be fitted with an adjustable collar to engage the edge of the grinding rest, and thus ensure that the tool's cutting point is guided in a direction parallel with the surface of the wheel.

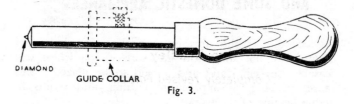

DIAMOND   GUIDE COLLAR

Fig. 3.

A diamond dressing tool of the type generally used for this purpose is depicted in Fig. 3.

As the diamond is harder than the abrasive material, it can be used to cut the wheel to run truly or to form it to any desired profile.

Nevertheless, if the abrasive grains are cut across, their cutting action will be less free than if they are crushed or fractured and left with a jagged surface.

Fig. 4.

Metal wheel-dressers, on the other hand, although too soft to cut the abrasive material, break up the surface of the wheel and expose fresh, sharp grains.

The Huntington star-wheel dressing tool, shown in Fig. 4, is probably the best-known pattern in common

Fig. 5.

use, but these tools are also made furnished with corrugated discs, as depicted in Fig. 5, for producing a rather finer surface finish to the wheel.

Hand tools are made for wheel-dressing and truing, similar in appearance to the diamond dresser, but carrying a stick of abrasive compound at the tip.

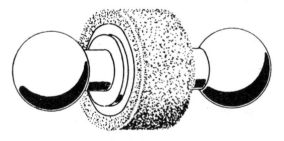

Fig. 6.

An abrasive wheel, mounted on a short shaft with a handle at either end, is also used for wheel dressing. The handles are in the form of cast-iron knobs to add weight and steady the appliance while in operation. The character of the surface, whether smooth or rough, imparted to the wheel can .be varied by altering the angle at which the device is held when in use. An appliance of this type is illustrated in Fig. 6.

B

CHAPTER II

SHARPENING APPLIANCES

ALTHOUGH both wood and metal-working tools are in many instances sharpened entirely by hand on the grinding wheel or bench stone, greater accuracy in the formation of the cutting edge can be obtained by using a guide, or jig, to maintain the tool in correct angular alignment with the surface of the abrasive stone or wheel.

With long practice, the carpenter is able to sharpen his tools free-hand to cut to his satisfaction, but this may be far from being the case where the novice is concerned.

Even the experienced mechanic can hardly be expected to grind a small twist drill by hand to that extreme degree of accuracy which is essential if the drill is to cut a hole truly aligned and exactly to size.

BENCH-STONE JIGS. Edged-tools such as wood chisels and plane irons, and also scrapers used for metal work, have their cutting edges formed by grinding away the tip of the tool to an angle. This angle varies with the use to which the tool is put, and although it should be as acute as possible to promote free-cutting, it must at the same time afford sufficient strength for the cutting edge to stand up to the work imposed. Thus, a greater or more obtuse angle is required for a firmer wood chisel, which is struck by a mallet, than is necessary for a paring chisel worked only by hand pressure. Again, the angle given to the metal scraping tool should be such that it does not tend to dig into the surface when applied to the work.

The most suitable angles for edged-tools have been

determined by long experience, and for wood-working tools, with which, for the moment, we are chiefly concerned, these lie between 25 and 45 deg.

In order that tools may be accurately sharpened to these angles, various jigs for use in connection with the bench stone have been devised. Fig. 7 shows a jig used

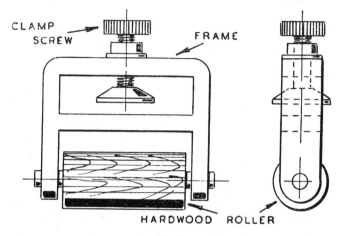

CLAMP
SCREW

FRAME

HARDWOOD ROLLER

Fig. 7.

for sharpening plane irons and wood chisels, and Fig. 8 illustrates the method of using the jig on the bench stone.

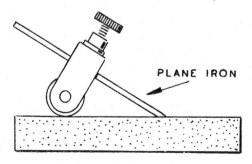

PLANE IRON

Fig. 8.

It will be apparent that the angle formed at the cutting
edge depends on the distance to which the tool is set out
from the clamp. Another device designed for similar
operations is depicted in Fig. 9, and, here, the angle honed
on the tool is adjusted by means of the screw that forms
part of the roller component.

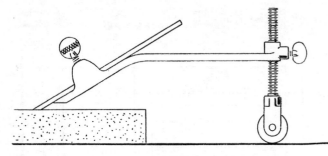

Fig. 9.

The most convenient method of setting the tool correctly
to the stone is, perhaps, by means of a template made of
cardboard, plastic material, or sheet metal, and for this
purpose, a set of templates should be cut to cover the
range of tool settings required. The sheet material can
be marked-out with a protractor and then cut and, if
necessary, filed to shape.

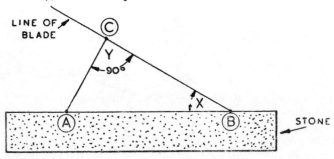

Fig. 10.

When a suitable protractor is not available for this purpose, the necessary dimensions can readily be calculated by the use of simple trigonometry. In Fig. 10 *AB* represents the surface of the stone, *CB* the line of the tool, and *X* the angle to be marked-out. The angle *Y* remains a right-angle throughout.

Now, if we take a piece of sheet material with two sides formed at a right-angle to represent the angle *Y*, and if we mark-off *CB* as, say, 4 in., then we have only to determine the length of *AC* to mark-out the angle *X* by joining the points *A* and *B*, and so complete the template.

In trigonometry the ratio of the length of *AC* to *CB* expressed as $\dfrac{AC}{CB}$, represents the tangent of the angle *X*, which we will assume to be 30 deg.

Reference to a set of tables will show that the tangent of an angle of 30 deg. is equal to 0.577.

If, therefore, *CB* = 4 in.

then *AC* = 0.577 × 4

= 2.308 in. or 2 5/16 in. will be sufficiently accurate for our purpose.

With a base *CB* of 4 in. the length of the perpendicular *AC* will be as shown in the following table.

Angle	Base	Perpendicular
deg.	in.	in.
25	4	1 $\frac{7}{8}$
30	4	2 5/16
35	4	2 51/64
40	4	3 23/64
45	4	4

When a tool has once been set by means of the template to the required angle, it can readily be reset on future occasions if the distance it projects from the clamping bracket is measured and recorded, but this particular setting only holds good, of course, for other tools having a blade of similar thickness.

Where the tip of the tool has its cutting edge formed nearly at right angles to the upper surface, as in the case of a lathe tool, it would be difficult to sharpen this edge with the tool held almost vertically, for digging-in into the surface of the stone would be liable to occur ; in this case, therefore, it is usually preferable to use a jig for guiding the *stone* whilst the tool is held stationary.

Fig. 11 and 12 illustrate a simple jig which can be used with advantage when stoning the tips of lathe, shaper, and planer tools.

Two steel side members, which support and guide the stone, are secured to a wooden base clamped to the bench top. These side-members are formed at one end to an angle of 5 deg. and at the other to 10 deg., so that the stone is tilted this amount while it is worked to and fro against the end cutting face of the tool. The tool is held in place on the baseboard with the fingers, and is moved forwards to maintain the tip in contact with the stone as the honing operation proceeds.

If the cutting edge has to be formed at right angles to

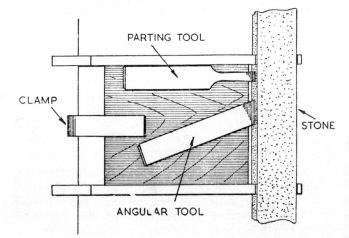

Fig. 11.

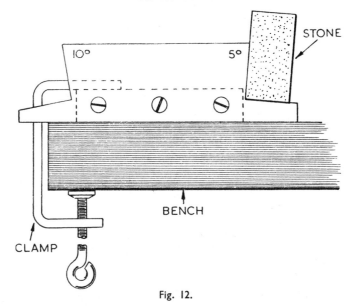

Fig. 12.

the length of the tool, as in the case of a parting tool, the tool is held in contact with the side-member as shown ; but where the tip is formed at an angle, a fence or guide piece can, if desired, be fitted to the baseboard to set and maintain the required alignment.

To stone a tool with a clearance angle of 10 deg., instead of the 5 deg. shown in the drawing, the jig is merely turned end for end.

The side members should be made of steel strip some $\frac{1}{4}$ in. thick to resist wear, and, as shown in the drawing, these components are provided with extended limbs to support the stone and to prevent it from rubbing against the bench top.

If desired, the G-clamp can be recessed into the upper surface of the baseboard so as not to encumber the surface of the tool rest.

GRINDING RESTS AND JIGS. These appliances are used

to obtain both ac-
curacy and unifor-
mity when grinding
tools, particularly
those used in pro-
duction work, where
consistent results
would not be pos-
sible if free-hand
methods of tool
sharpening were ad-
opted.

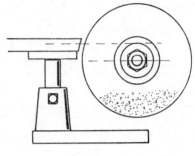

Fig. 13.

Lathe tools may,
of course, be hand ground on occasion, but as a regular
practice it is better to use some form of guide, which
will ensure that the tool is presented to form the cutting
edge correctly.

Many forms of adjustable grinding rests are fitted to
grinding heads, some are intended for grinding the work
on the periphery of the wheel, and others are designed for
use in connection with its side surfaces.

When the periphery of the wheel is used, the rest is
set so that the centre line of the tool lies a little above the
wheel centre, in order to form the necessary clearance
angle on the front
face of the tool. Ref-
erence to Fig. 13
should make this
point clear ; and it
will be seen that
the above-centre
height of the table is
adjusted by raising
and lowering the
rest vertically. The
same result can be
obtained, as shown
in Fig. 14, where it

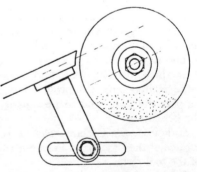

Fig. 14.

will be seen the table can be tilted, and at the same time adjusted at the correct distance from the wheel, by means of a clamp-bolt sliding in a slot in the supporting arm.

It will be apparent that, as set out diagrammatically in Fig. 15, a different height adjustment is required for large and small tools ; for, while the height of the rest at *A* is correct for grinding a large tool, the small tool at *B* has its centre line below the wheel centre line, and so would be ground with a negative front clearance that would cause it merely to rub against the work.

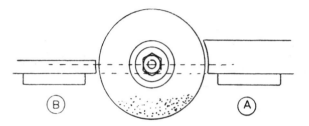

Fig. 15.

The pillar of the vertically adjustable rest can readily be graduated for grinding tools of various thicknesses, and also for altering the size of the clearance angle formed ; but in the case of the tilting and sliding-rest the matter is more involved, and setting the rest by means of a template against the surface of the wheel may be found a more satisfactory method.

When a grinding rest provided with a means of angular adjustment is used, such as that illustrated in Fig. 16, the angular grinding of tools is greatly facilitated by using the side faces of the wheel, and the exact height of the tool in relation to the wheel centre is then immaterial Rests of this type can be readily graduated and furnished with a scale and pointer for setting the angularity ; or, if preferred, a sheet-metal template can be used for

Fig. 16.

this purpose. In addition to the commercial types of grinding rests described, the rest illustrated in Fig. 17, which was designed to meet personal requirements, may also be found useful.

This grinding rest has the advantages that it can be adjusted for both angularity and height to enable it to be used in relation either to the side or the periphery of the grinding wheel ; and, moreover, the grinding table can, if desired, be replaced by one of a form suitable for cutter grinding or other special work. At its lower end the vertical arm carries a spindle which is clamped in a bracket attached to the bench top.

This bracket is similar to that used to carry the Potts drill grinding jig, and its adoption in this instance allows either the grinding-rest or the drill grinder to be used at will, and, furthermore, the change-over can be easily and quickly made.

As will be seen in the drawing, a sole-plate *A*, for attachment to the bench, carries a vertical spindle *B*, which forms a pivot for the clamping piece *C*. This split clamp, into which the spindle *D* of the rest fits, is closed by means of a lever clamp nut *E*, and a locking bolt *F* is provided to prevent the clamping piece from turning on its pivot after the components have been correctly set.

It will be apparent that the spindle *D* can rotate in the component *C*, in order to set the rest to the wheel, and in addition, it can slide endways for adjusting the gap in

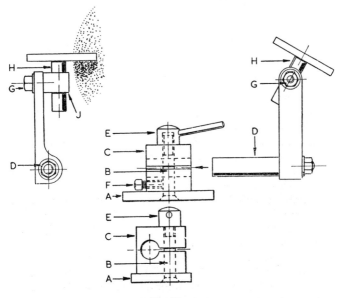

Fig. 17.

the grinding table to clear the sides of the grinding wheel. When the nut *G* is slackened, the pillar *H* of the grinding table can slide in the sleeved-clamp collar *J*, to afford height adjustment, and at the same time the table can be tilted to the exact angle required for grinding the tool. If desired, the vertical limb supporting the rest can be graduated and a pointer can be attached to the clamp-collar spindle to indicate the angular setting of the grinding table.

GRINDING MACHINES. The simplest type of grinding head, which could formerly be purchased for a few shillings, consists of an iron casting with integral bearings to carry the wheel spindle. The latter are split and closed by screws to afford some measure of adjustment to counter-act wear.

Needless to say, at this low price neither the bearings nor the shaft could be precision fitted ; but if the bearings are rebored, reamed, and finally lapped, and a lapped alloy steel shaft is accurately fitted, the outcome will be a very serviceable grinding head for light work.

Moreover, if a single wheel is used and a pulley is fitted to the other extremity of the shaft, two such machines, driven by a common electric motor can be employed to mount a coarse and a fine wheel for rough and finish grinding respectively.

The change-over is made by merely changing the belt and, if desired, one machine can be made to slide to one side when not in use in order to give better access to the other.

As these simple machines do not carry grinding rests, a grinding table must be improvised and secured to the bench top in a position to serve the machine. The grinding rest illustrated in Fig. 17 will be found eminently suitable for this purpose.

The more elaborate and therefore more expensive grinding machines are robustly constructed and may be fitted with ball bearings to render them suitable for long, continuous running without attention ; also, where the belt-drive is taken from the lineshafting, fast and loose pulleys with a belt-shifting gear are fitted.

As already indicated, various types of grinding rests are fitted to these machines, and some have provision for fitting a drill grinding jig ; the spindle is usually double-ended and carries two wheels suitable for rough and finish tool grinding.

In some cases, a self-contained type of machine may be preferred which has the advantage that it can be moved from place to place as required. These machines comprise an electric motor, with an extended armature-shaft carrying a grinding wheel at either end. The motor is wound to run at a speed suitable for the wheels fitted, and is controlled by a switch mounted on the body of the machine.

Grinding rests are also fitted, and in some instances a drill-grinding jig can be supplied as an extra attachment ; in addition, some makes of machine are adapted for attaching a flexible shaft to the spindle for driving small cutting tools or abrasive wheels and pencils ; the latter will be found useful for sharpening small tools such as screw-threading dies.

As mentioned in the previous chapter, small India wheels will be found useful for grinding pointed tools and fine boring tools, where only a minimum of metal has to be removed in order to preserve the tool's original form. These wheels can be conveniently mounted on the spindle of a small electric motor, such as a fan-motor, which can usually be acquired at small cost, but as fan motors are generally series-wound, their speed must be controlled by means of the series resistance switch with which they are fitted.

A simplified form of the grinding rest, illustrated in Fig. 17 should be attached to the baseboard on which the motor is mounted.

MOUNTING GRINDING WHEELS. When mounting the wheel, the lead bush fitted to its centre should be an easy sliding fit on the grinding machine spindle, and any high spots found in the bore, which prevent a free fit, should be carefully removed by scraping with the blade of a sharp knife.

The wheel itself is supported between two flanges, the inner of which should be securely fixed to the spindle and turned to run true when in place.

These flanges must be relieved, as shown in Fig. 18, and the pressure they exert on the wheel should be evenly distributed at the outer diameter by interposing washers of blotting paper, or other soft material, between them and the faces of the wheel.

For general use, the diameter of these flanges should be equal to half the diameter of the wheel, but for light

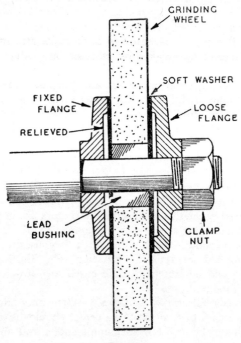

Fig. 18.

grinding rather smaller flanges may be employed, provided that, when grinding, no excessive side-thrust is imparted to the wheel.

The wheel is secured in place by means of a clamping nut, which must be tightened no more than is necessary to afford an adequate frictional driving grip on the wheel.

When the wheel is arranged, as it should be, to rotate towards the operator, the screw-thread at the right of the spindle must be right-handed, but left-handed at the other extremity if a wheel is mounted in that position ; otherwise, the nut will tend to slacken and the wheel may become loose.

If, when the wheel has been secured in place on the spindle, it is found to run slightly out of truth, it must be trued by means of a diamond tool or a metal disc wheel dresser, as described in Chapter I.

These tools should be used with care and not crowded on to the wheel ; only light cuts must be taken, and the tool is worked across the wheel in a straight line by keeping the adjustable guide collar in contact with the edge of the grinding table.

CHAPTER III

SHARPENING METALWORKING TOOLS

LATHE TOOLS. In the small workshop the sharpening of the turning tools is a matter of the greatest importance, and one which the tyro often finds the most difficult ; nevertheless, on it very largely depends the accuracy and the general quality of the lathe work undertaken.

A blunt or incorrectly sharpened tool may well cause undue heating and distortion of the work, as well as a ragged and torn surface finish.

Those who perforce rely on foot power for operating the lathe soon learn to their cost that an increased output of energy is required to operate a blunt tool, or one that has its cutting edges incorrectly formed ; but, on the other hand, they quickly come to appreciate the value of a properly sharpened tool.

Although in factories a high rate of output must be maintained by working robust tools up to their maximum capacity consistent with accuracy, in the small workshop the operator may seek rather to obtain results of high quality irrespective of the time spent, and for this reason he forms his turning tools to give free-cutting and a good surface finish.

Some workers never advance beyond the stage of grinding their lathe tools by the free-hand method and trusting to the eye to determine the form of the tool. Although many may find this procedure perfectly satisfactory, there is much to be said for the accuracy and uniformity obtained when an adjustable form of tool-rest or grinding jig is used to set the cutting angles automatically.

Before going further, it may be helpful to examine in detail the more common tool forms in general use.

The shape of the tool-tip presented to the work is determined by the angles to which the cutting edges are ground, and although these will vary in their disposition in accordance with the purpose for which the tool is used, they will, nevertheless, remain substantially of the same value in all tools used for machining any particular material.

The essential angles concerned in a tool's formation are termed clearance and rake angles.

THE CLEARANCE ANGLE. Wherever the cutting edge of the lathe tool comes in contact with the work, clearance must be provided behind this edge to ensure that it alone makes contact with the work surface ; otherwise, the tool will tend merely to rub and will not cut freely.

In Fig. 19A, where the tool is viewed from the position of the tailstock, the front clearance between the tip of the tool and the work surface is shown ; whilst, when looking along the tool from the front of the lathe, the side-clearance provided in the direction of the tool's travel is illustrated in Fig. 19B.

The clearance angle, then, is not concerned with the actual cutting process, but merely ensures that the cutting edge alone makes contact with the work.

THE RAKE ANGLE. In this case, the tool surfaces concerned are those against which the chips impinge as they are sheared from the work surface. Further reference to Figs. 19A and B will show that the top rake is the angle of the backward slope of the tool's upper surface from the front cutting edge. Likewise, the side rake is the angular slope away from the work in relation to the side-cutting edge.

THE KNIFE TOOL. The tool shown in Fig. 19A, B and C is a typical knife tool, and when it is formed to cut towards the headstock of the lathe it is termed right-handed, and when in the reverse direction left-handed.

C

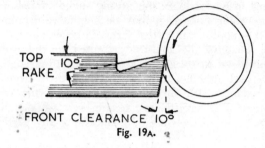

Fig. 19A.

Although top rake has been shown for the purpose of illustration, it is not essential, and is often omitted, in order that the height of the cutting edge may remain nearly constant as the tool is resharpened.

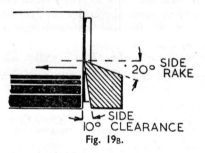

Fig. 19B.

The clearance and rake angles indicated are suitable for a tool used to turn mild-steel to a good finish, either when being traversed along the work or when facing a surface. Although in a tool of this pattern the whole width of the front face might be presented to the work, this would probably cause chatter and an inaccurate finish, due to the great pressure exerted on the work by the large area of contact.

It is usual, therefore, to form the tip of the tool as shown in Fig. 19c, so that the width of the cutting edge is much reduced by imparting what is termed relief behind the point of contact. However, to give a good finish to the work, the end of the tool should either be slightly rounded or have a small flat stoned at the extreme tip. Moreover, it will be apparent that when the tip of the tool has a rounded form it will give a good finish to the work both when traversing and facing.

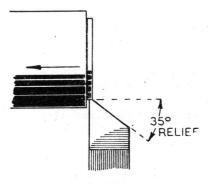

Fig. 19c.

THE PARTING TOOL. The same principles are applied in the case of the parting tool, illustrated in Fig. 20, but here the angles of clearance, rake and relief are somewhat reduced, in order to maintain the strength of this more slender but highly-stressed tool.

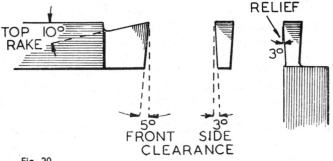

Fig. 20.

The tool depicted is suitable for parting mild steel, but for use on brass and similar alloys no top rake should be given, otherwise digging into the work is apt to occur.

THE BORING TOOL.   The illustration in Fig. 21A of a boring tool in operation shows that ample front clearance must be given, to prevent the heel of the tool from rubbing against the bore when small holes are being machined.

When grinding the tool to shape, it is a good plan to enter it in a hole in the drill-gauge to make sure that this clearance is adequate for the size of the hole to be bored.

In addition, the leading edge of the tool must be provided with side clearance, as shown in Fig. 21B.   The top rake is determined by the angle the upper surface of the tool makes with the diameter of the circle within which it operates, and this rake can be set as required either by adjusting the height of the tool or by rotating it when it is held in a split clamping block.

Side-rake is necessary when machining steel in order to promote free-cutting.

As shown in Fig. 21C, slender boring tools should have ample relief behind the cutting edge to reduce the pressure on the tool tip and prevent it from springing away from the work.

Tools of forms other than those illustrated should be

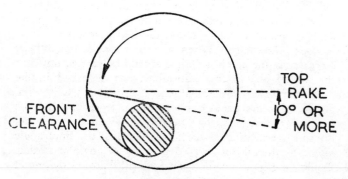

Fig. 21A.

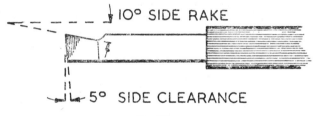

Fig. 21B.

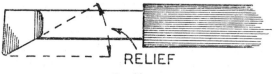

Fig. 21c.

ground to the same equivalent angles for use on mild steel, but for turning brass alloys it is usual to give no top-rake and, also, to reduce the clearance angles ; however, it may be found that in some instances better work results when a small amount of top-rake is provided, if at the same time chatter and digging-in can be avoided.

Although only a few standard angles have been instanced, it may be found that better results can be obtained with individual lathes, and when machining different materials, if these angles are varied somewhat, but in all cases experiment will be found the best guide.

Tool Grinding. When the tool angles have been decided on, the actual grinding should be carried out with the aid of one of the adjustable rests described in the previous chapter, and, as a general principle, less material should be removed as the operation proceeds from the rough to the finished stage, in order to lessen the work and prevent overheating of the tool. Thus, if the final angle honed by the oilstone is 10 deg., then an angle of 12 deg. should be ground on the coarse wheel, followed by one of 11 deg. on the fine wheel.

To facilitate setting the angular rest, templates of the form shown in Fig. 22, and made of plastic material or sheet-metal can be used with advantage ; whilst to maintain the template in a vertical position on the work table it should be mounted in a rule holder or supported against a metal block.

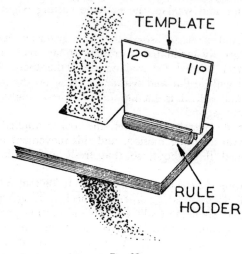

Fig. 22.

For the sake of convenience, a set of templates should be made to cover the range of angles required for the various tool forms used.

Although these templates are in every way suitable for setting the angular grinding rest correctly in relation to the side faces of the wheel, some difficulty may be experienced when they are used to adjust the height of a rest relative to the periphery of the wheel. In the latter case, as has been pointed out, the setting of the rest will vary with the thickness of the tool and with the diameter of the wheel when a constant clearance angle is required.

It follows, therefore, that if tools of three different

thicknesses are to be ground by the latter method, on wheels of two different diameters, six sets of templates will be required to meet all eventualities.

Moreover, when a large grinding wheel of say 12-in. diam. is employed, the curvatures formed on the faces of the tool will be nearly linear, but with a small wheel of only 3 or 4 in. diam., the concavities ground may seriously undermine and weaken the extreme cutting edges of the tool.

It should be emphasised that the grinding operation will be greatly facilitated if ground, square section, high-speed steel is used for making the lathe tools, for this material will lie flat and without rocking on the grinding table, and will thus enable the required angles to be accurately ground.

When the rest has been set, the tool is applied to the wheel with a sliding motion, and this movement must be maintained throughout, so that fresh surfaces are constantly brought to bear on the wheel, and the risk of overheating the steel is thus reduced. If the tool is allowed to dwell or is forced against the wheel, heating will arise which may spoil the tool's temper and cutting properties. On no account should the tool be dipped in water to accelerate cooling, for the subsequent evaporation of the water during grinding may cause surface cracks to form at the cutting edge.

When the cutting edges have been satisfactorily formed on the coarse wheel, the work is transferred to the fine or finishing wheel, and if, as already explained, the grinding rest is set to form a slightly smaller clearance angle, it will be found that but little further grinding is required to impart a good finish to the cutting edge, and at the same time there is very little risk of overheating the tool.

STONING THE TOOL. On completion of the grinding operations, the final finish is given to the cutting edges of the tool on the oilstone. If free-hand stoning is employed, great care must be taken to avoid rounding the tool's edges and thereby reducing their clearance angles.

With this possibility in view, it is better, whenever possible, to use a stoning jig of the pattern described in the previous chapter, and if the tool has been ground in the manner indicated, it can usually be resharpened several times on the oilstone before regrinding becomes necessary.

It is essential that a hard stone, such as an Arkansas oilstone, should be used for this purpose, for if the tool cuts into and grooves the surface of the stone, a rounded or even a blunted cutting edge may result. Light pressure only should be applied when honing and the stone should be kept clean and well lubricated.

HAND-TURNING TOOLS. Before leaving the subject of sharpening lathe tools, two tools commonly used in hand turning should be mentioned, namely the graver and the thread-chasing tool.

THE GRAVER. When mounted in a wooden handle and supported on the handrest, the graver, illustrated in Fig. 23, is used for a great variety of hand-turning operations.

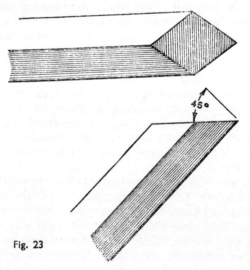

Fig. 23

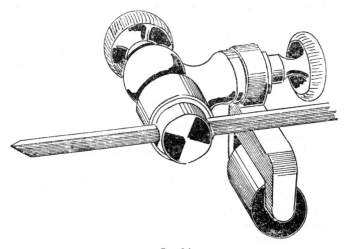

Fig. 24.

As will be seen, the point is ground at an angle of 45 deg. to the long axis of the tool to form a lozenge-shaped facet, thus forming two cutting edges at the sides of the pointed tip. The tool is best ground by supporting it in a V-block on the table of the angular grinding rest, which is tilted to form an angle of 45 deg. with the side-face of the grinding wheel. The sides of the tool should on no account be ground, and great care must be exercised when grinding not to overheat and soften the slender tip.

After grinding, the flat area at the tip should be honed to a highly finished surface on the oilstone, and for this purpose, the use of a stoning jig will be found a great advantage.

A convenient form of stoning jig is illustrated in Fig. 24, but the jig described for stoning plane irons in the previous chapter can also be used, if a recess to receive the shank of the graver is filed in the surface of the clamping piece.

When the surface of the lozenge-shaped facet has been accurately honed, the sharpening operation is completed by applying the sides of the graver flat to the stone, and with a few light, well controlled strokes removing any burrs that may have been formed at the cutting edges.

HAND CHASERS. Chasers are essentially form-tools and may be used, when mounted in a wooden handle and

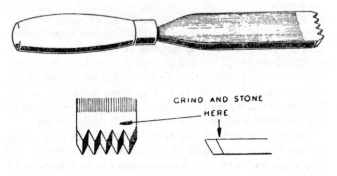

GRIND AND STONE HERE

Fig. 25.

supported on the hand rest, to give the correct form and final fit to threads screwcut in the lathe. It will usually be found that the upper surface of the tool is flat and in direct continuation of the shank of the chaser. This indicates that, in order to preserve it as a form-tool, the upper surface must be ground or stoned in precisely this manner, otherwise the shape of the cutting teeth will be altered and the tool will no longer serve its intended purpose.

When grinding is required, the upper surface of the end portion of the tool is applied to the side of the wheel, after which the chaser is laid flat on the oilstone and is then moved backwards and forwards in the direction of its long axis, after the manner of stoning the back of a wood chisel.

On no account must the front face of the chaser be allowed to come in contact with the grinding wheel, or the tool will be spoilt for the purpose of thread finishing.

The ordinary form of hand-chaser designed for external work is depicted in Fig. 25, and for internal chasing the teeth are cut on the side of the tool which is then akin in form to a boring tool.

At this point, an unusual method of grinding an external chaser to serve a special purpose might, perhaps, be mentioned.

When some ribbed tread-plate was required for the cabin floor of a model steam-roller under construction, an $\frac{1}{8}$-in. pitch chaser was ground on its end face, with a clearance angle of 10 deg., until the teeth were almost obliterated and only the shallow hollows between the teeth remained. This tool was then mounted in the shaping machine, and a strip of tread-plate with raised ribs was machined equal to the breadth of the chaser.

The work was then traversed for a distance equal to the number of the teeth of the chaser by means of the $\frac{1}{8}$-in. pitch feed screw, and the process was continued until the full width of the plate had been machined. The result of this improvised operation was most satisfactory and the appearance fully realistic.

In this short review of the subject of sharpening lathe tools, attention has been paid rather to the general principles involved than to listing the many varieties of tools, and the cutting angles recommended, for turning the numerous materials commonly used in the workshop.

In general, these angles are not critical except, perhaps, where maximum output is required ; and satisfactory work should result if the tool is given sufficient clearance to prevent rubbing ; adequate rake to promote free-cutting ; relief to prevent too large an area of contact with the work ; and a form to provide proper support for the cutting edges.

Lathe tools can readily be endowed with all these qualities by adopting the methods of sharpening described.

Finally, it is necessary to emphasise that turning tools should always be kept really sharp, that is to say in the sense that a knife capable of free-cutting is said to be sharp.

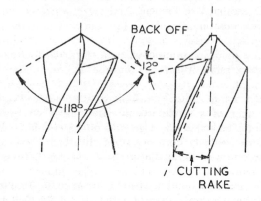

Fig. 26.

TWIST AND STRAIGHT-FLUTE DRILLS. The form of a general purpose twist drill is shown in Fig. 26, and sharpening is carried out by grinding the two conical portions of the tip lying behind the cutting lips.

The included angle at the tip is usually ground to 118 deg., and the clearance angle of 12 deg. behind the cutting edge is formed by a method of conical backing-off.

The two spiral flutes which give the drill its name impart a rake to the cutting edges. In the straight-flute drill, on the other hand, although the formation of the tip is similar, there is no rake at the cutting edges.

When sharpening a twist drill, it is essential that both the angularity and the length of the two lips should be similar, and that the backing-off to form the clearance angles for the cutting edges should be equal ; otherwise, if one lip is longer than the other an over-size hole will be drilled, and if the drilling pressure is not borne equally by the two cutting edges, the drill point will not follow a straight course.

Although a lathe tool may be ground successfully free-hand by the skilled operator, it will be apparent that the accurate sharpening of a twist drill is a much more difficult matter, even when a reference gauge is used to assist the operation.

If accurate drilling is to be expected, a grinding jig should be used, in conjunction with the grinding machine, when sharpening drills.

A typical small grinding jig, the Potts, which will hold drills of from $\frac{1}{16}$ in. to $\frac{1}{2}$ in. diam., is shown in Fig. 27.

This appliance is carried in a base bracket which is secured to the bench-top adjacent to the grinding machine, and, as has already been described, this bracket may also be used to mount an angular grinding rest as an alternative attachment.

The angular inclination of the main pivot is designed to impart the standard angle of 118 deg. to the drill point, and when the drill carrier is rotated on this pivot the correct conical back-off is ground on the cutting lips.

In order to adjust the amount of the back-off formed, in correct relation to the size of the drill, the drill carrier is made to slide on the head of the pivot, so that the drill point can be set to protrude a definite distance beyond the axis of rotation of the pivot.

The correct amount by which the carrier is advanced beyond the pivot axis is set by means of a pair of calliper

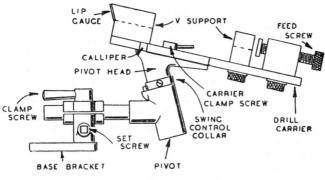

Fig 27.

jaws ; the fixed jaw forms part of the pivot head and the sliding jaw is attached to the drill carrier.

When the calliper is set by using the drill shank as a gauge, the jig is automatically set to form the correct degree of back-off for that particular drill.

To use the appliance ; after the horizontal spindle has been set parallel with the grinding spindle axis and then secured by tightening the bracket set-screw, the calliper jaws are closed on the drill shank and the carrier clamping screw is tightened.

The whole appliance is then moved forward in the base bracket until the head of the drill carrier is just clear of the surface of the grinding wheel. This latter operation is, perhaps, most readily carried out by interposing a piece of sheet metal, some 10/1000 of an inch in thickness, between the head and the wheel, and then locking the base bracket clamp screw when contact has been established.

If this procedure is followed there will be no danger of the wheel damaging the jig during the grinding operation, and the overhang of the drill point will be kept constant.

The drill is now placed in the V-blocks of the carrier with one lip in contact with the lip gauge, and with the tail of the carrier swung towards the left. When the wheel has been started, the feed-screw is turned until the point of the drill comes into light contact with the surface of the wheel, and while the drill is held in place with the fingers of the left hand, the carrier is swung slowly towards the right to the limit of its travel. The drill is now turned over to grind the other lip and the carrier is again rotated.

While the drill is in this position, the 40-t.p.i. feed-screw is turned some sixth of a revolution to advance the drill approximately 4/1000 of an inch, and the carrier is again operated as before. The drill is then once more turned over, and these operations are repeated until the whole surface of the drill point is evenly ground.

Straight-flute drills are ground in a similar manner, but when sharpening the points of centre drills, the correct setting of the calliper gauge must be determined by a process of trial and error to ensure that the proper amount of back-off is obtained.

Similarly, when grinding drills for special purposes, the amount of back-off can be increased or diminished at will by adjustment of the calliper setting.

Certain precautions should be observed when grinding drills ; the side-face of the grinding wheel must be truly flat, true running, and in good cutting condition, neither

STONE

GRIND

Fig. 28.

loaded with metal particles, nor glazed and blunted ; the drill must be fed forward very slowly, and only light cuts should be taken in order to prevent damage to the wheel and overheating of the drill point ; the drill carrier should be rotated slowly, but resolutely, and without dwell ; a second passage of the drill across the wheel, and without increasing the feed, will improve the finish of the work.

D-Bits. These tools are used for drilling or boring holes truly straight and accurately to size, but, to achieve this, they must be given guidance, at starting, in a bore machined to size, and of a depth equal to at least half the diameter of the bit. D-bits are readily made from silver steel, which can be purchased in lengths accurately ground to size.

As will be seen in the illustration in Fig. 28, the tool is formed to a D-section to provide a front cutting edge, which, as shown in Fig. 29, has both a front clearance and a relief of 5 deg.

Although, in theory, the upper face of the D-sectioned portion should lie on the diameter of the tool, in practice,

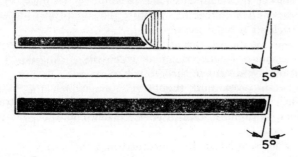

Fig. 29.

the depth of the tip is made greater than the half-diameter to prevent the bit from cutting oversize, and also to allow for stoning when resharpening becomes necessary.

The value of this allowance, which it is customary to provide, is shown in the drawing in Fig. 30, and, as will be apparent, this increases relatively to the diameter of the bit.

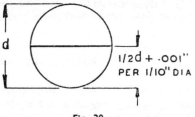

Fig. 30.

In the first instance, the D-bit is ground both on its flat upper face, and on the front cutting edge to the form depicted ; the upper face is then finished on the oilstone to the required diameter, whilst the front cutting edge is best sharpened by using a stoning jig of the type described and illustrated in the previous chapter.

To resharpen the tool, if possible the front face only should be stoned, for if the upper surface is frequently treated in this way, the critical allowance in excess of the diameter will be lost, and the efficiency of the tool will be impaired.

COUNTERBORES. These cutters, sometimes called pin drills, although commonly employed to form recesses for the heads of cheese-headed screws, are useful for many other operations such as spot-facing bolt-head seatings.

The usual two- and four-lipped forms with integral centre-pin are depicted in Fig. 31, but if this pin is made

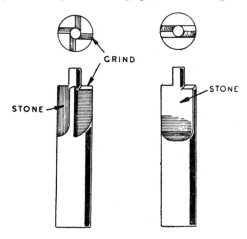

Fig. 31.

detachable, not only will the work of sharpening the cutting edges be facilitated, but the size of the guide-pin can be altered at will to suit the diameter of the hole drilled in the work.

If these tools are much used, it will be an advantage to make a simple grinding jig that will present the cutting edges at the correct angle to the grinding wheel, and will, at the same time, index the position of the lips to enable them to be ground equally. As an alternative, quite good results can be obtained by clamping the tool in a V-block, with its lips lying horizontally, and then tilting the grinding

D

table to grind the cutting edges with a clearance angle behind them. In addition, to maintain the V-block at right angles to the side-face of the wheel, a guide strip may be clamped temporarily to the surface of the grinding table.

On the other hand, if due care is taken, hand sharpening may be found quite satisfactory. If the cutting edges are badly worn they should be reshaped on the grinding wheel. The progress of the work can be readily checked by mounting the cutter in the drilling machine and pressing it, while stationary, against a piece of flat brass on the machine table ; the indentations made in the brass will then show clearly any inaccuracy or uneven bearing of the cutting edges. When a satisfactory result has been obtained, the sharpening operation should be completed by using an oilstone slip, and by this means, too, any burring of the cutting edges should be removed from the vertical faces of the tool.

In the case of the two-lipped cutter, the flat vertical faces can be more readily stoned when resharpening is required, but care must be taken not to form flats on the centre-pin and thereby reduce the guidance it is intended to afford.

In the cross-section of the cutter shown in the drawings it will be seen that no appreciable clearance or relief has been given behind the periphery of the cutting edges, for, as the tool is intended to cut only in the direction of its long axis, this is unnecessary except in so far as to prevent binding in the case of a worn cutter operating in a deep hole. When additional relief is required in this situation, it can be provided by careful hand stoning.

END MILLS AND SLOTTING CUTTERS. These tools, unlike the counterbore, are formed to cut laterally, that is to say in a direction at right angles to their long axis ; for this purpose additional cutting edges are provided as shown in Fig. 32, which depicts the common form of two-lipped slot mill.

In passing, it should be mentioned that cutters of this

type are readily made as required from silver steel, and
when used as end mills they are free-cutting and, unlike
the multi-lipped variety they have no tendency to become
clogged with swarf.

These tools are ground and sharpened in the same way
as counterbores but additional care is required to ensure
that the sides of the lips, as well as their end faces, cut
equally, and for this purpose, again, the use of a grinding
jig will greatly facilitate the sharpening operation.

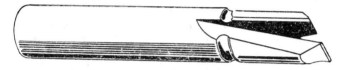

Fig. 32.

COUNTERSINKS.   Six different forms of these tools in
common use are illustrated, all of which are primarily
intended for forming a recessed conical seating to receive
the head of a countersunk screw.   Standard screws used for
both metal and woodwork, such as those manufactured by
Messrs. Nettlefold, are made with an included angle of
90 deg., but to ensure that the heads of these countersunk
screws seat correctly by making contact with the work at
their greatest diameter, countersinks, and particularly
those made for woodworking, are usually made with their
cutting edges to include an angle of rather less than 90
deg.   However, countersinks can also be readily obtained
with an included angle of 60 deg., and these, together with
the familiar Slocombe centre drill, are used, amongst
other purposes, for the preparation of work to engage the
conical centres of the lathe.

The Snailhorn form of countersink shown in Fig. 33A
is generally made for seating wood screws, but the better
makes, which are hardened and tempered, are also useful
for metalwork as they cut freely and have but little tendency to chatter, if run sufficiently slowly.   The cutting

A
(WOOD)

B
(WOOD)

C
(WOOD)
NOT WORTH THE TROUBLE
OF RESHARPENING

Fig. 33.

edges are sharpened as indicated in the drawing by using a tapered oilstone or India slip. Should the tool become much worn with prolonged use, the metal behind the two cutting edges should be relieved by careful grinding.

The two-lipped wood countersink, illustrated in Fig. 33B, as made by Messrs. Starrett, is hardened and ground and will, therefore, but rarely require sharpening. This model has a rather wider gap than is shown in the drawing, and ample space is provided for using a triangular oilstone slip when resharpening the cutting edges.

The Rosehead countersink, Fig. 33C, costs but a few pence and is so roughly made that it does not invite resharpening.

The pattern shown in Fig. 33D, however, has fewer cutting edges, but these are accurately ground and the

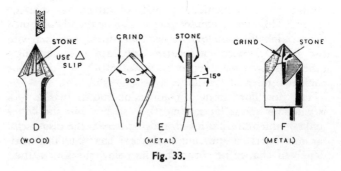

D
(WOOD)

E
(METAL)

F
(METAL)

Fig. 33.

teeth are not so liable to become clogged. To resharpen the tool, the leading faces of the cutting edges are honed with a triangular oilstone or India slip. Any attempt to grind the periphery of the cutter may result in damaging the following cutting edge, but careful hand stoning may be used, provided that the clearance or relief behind the cutting edges is not unduly reduced.

The spear-headed countersink depicted in Fig. 33E was formerly employed for metalworking, but as it is very liable to chatter it is now seldom used. Nevertheless, it can be very easily resharpened, as illustrated, and the included angle can be readily altered by grinding to suit any particular purpose.

The cutting lips are ground with a clearance of some 15 deg., by using the angular grinding rest, and the angle included at the point is checked with a suitable gauge or protractor. The cutting edges should be finished by honing the flat sides on the oilstone.

The four-lipped metal countersink, Fig. 33F, will be found prone to chatter unless firmly supported and run slowly.

The radial faces leading the cutting edges can be stoned to resharpen the tool, but as there is but little bearing surface towards the tip to guide the stone, great care must be taken to avoid rounding the cutting edges and thus impairing their cutting properties. The peripheral surface of the cutting edges can be ground free-hand, nearly up to the actual cutting edge, and this surface is then finished with a hand stone.

Care must be taken, however, to maintain the proper clearance angles and also not to upset the line of the cutting edges.

A non-chattering type of metal countersink is illustrated in Fig. 33G. Here, only one lip actually cuts while the other acts as a guide and steady.

Once the tool has been formed as shown in the drawing, resharpening is carried out by stoning the flat face, but should this surface be reduced to lie below the line of the diameter, the tool's non-chattering properties will be lost.

In the drawing the dimension to which the point is ground is shown as $\dfrac{d}{2}$, where d is the diameter, to which is added an allowance of 1/1000 of an inch for each 1/10 of an inch of the tool's diameter. This addition is made to allow for the removal of metal when resharpening, and in the case of a ½-in. diam countersink it would, therefore, amount to 5/1000 of an inch.

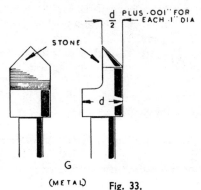

Fig. 33.

Should the tool be found not to cut freely, slight relief may be given behind the cutting edge by using an oilstone slip, but if this is carried to excess the tool will tend to chatter.

REAMERS. The end portion of a parallel straight-fluted reamer is shown in Fig. 34, and a drawing depicting the tooth form in section is given in Fig. 35A.

Hand reamers are usually tapered towards the point for a short distance to give a lead into the hole at the start of the reaming operation. During manufacture, and after the flutes have been milled in the tool blank, the reamer is hardened and tempered before the final grinding to size over the crests of the teeth.

This process is carried out with extreme accuracy in

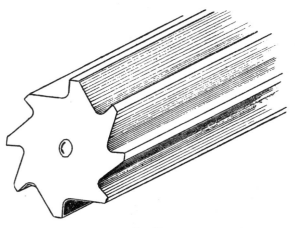

Fig. 34.

a grinding machine specially equipped for the purpose, and its repetition is usually beyond the resources of the small workshop. Moreover, were the crests of the teeth reground in this way, the diameter of the tool would be reduced, and it would not then cut to its full nominal size.

Fig. 35B illustrates the result of extreme wear, and it will be seen that the sharp crests forming the cutting edges have been worn away to form flat surfaces that will merely rub, and not cut, the internal surface of the hole into which the reamer has been introduced.

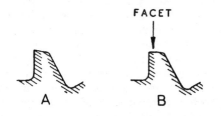

FACET

A   B

Fig. 35.

To maintain a reamer in good working condition, the crests of the teeth should be examined periodically and at the first sign of the formation of a rubbing area an oilstone slip should be used as indicated in Fig. 36. It is essential that a hard stone, such as an Arkansas should be used, for if a soft stone is employed its surface will be grooved and the cutting edges of the reamer will become rounded and in effect blunted.

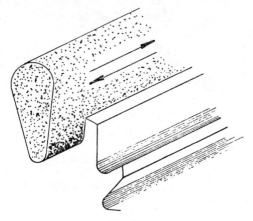

Fig. 36.

If, from time to time, resharpening is carried out, the useful life of the reamer will be greatly prolonged, and its effective diameter will be but little reduced.

Should large rubbing surfaces have formed at the crests of the teeth, due to neglect of these precautions, an attempt may be made, as a matter of expediency, to restore the reamer's lost cutting properties by hand stoning the crests of the teeth behind the cutting edges, but great care must be taken to treat the lips equally and also to maintain adequate clearance to allow the cutting edges to operate.

It is, however, usually better to have the reamer re-ground by an expert once it has become seriously blunted.

It should be emphasised that a common cause of blunting reamers is the practice of turning the tool in the reverse direction when withdrawing it from the work ; reamers must always be turned only in the forward or cutting direction, and should be kept well lubricated with lard oil when used to cut ferrous metals.

Reamers may sometimes be found to cut oversize when new ; in such an event, if a correctly-sized hole is required, hand stoning the crests of the teeth will be necessary, and should be carried out as described, until a trial shows that the tool cuts to its exact nominal size.

Adjustable reamers, of either the inset-blade or expanding type, should be reground by an expert craftsman as soon as their free-cutting properties become impaired, otherwise they are of little use for carrying out the exact sizing operations usually required of them.

DIES. In the familiar form of circular split-die illustrated in Fig. 37, it will be seen that the cutting edges are formed at the points where the chip clearance holes break into the threaded bore. Although this method of

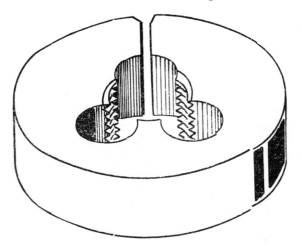

Fig. 37.

construction, which is
shown in greater de-
tail in Fig. 38, ensures
that in a new die
the cutting edges are
sharp and free-cutting,
with use these edges
in time become blun-
ted and resharpening
will then be necessary.

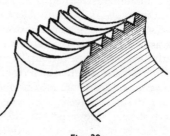

Fig. 38.

The cutting edges
of the die can be restored by working with a pencil-shaped
abrasive slip in the clearance holes, as depicted in Fig.
39, but this is a slow process, and more rapid results can
be obtained by using a pencil hone, driven by an electric
hand tool.

Alternatively, the hone may be attached to a flexible
drive-shaft connected to an electric motor, as in the case of
the all too familiar dentist's drill. During the grinding
operation, the die is held in the hand and worked backwards

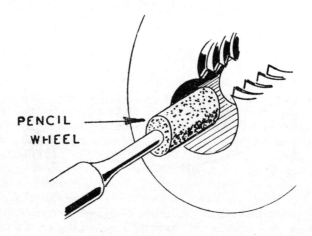

PENCIL
WHEEL

Fig. 39.

and forwards as the cutting edges are brought to bear on the rotating hone.

TAPS. The cutting edges of blunted taps can, in some measure, be restored by using an oilstone slip in the manner described for resharpening reamers. It should be noted that, as shown in Fig. 40, the lips of the tap are usually rather more undercut and have more cutting-rake than

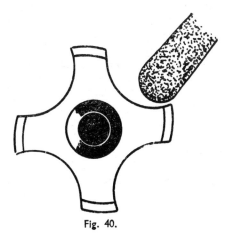

Fig. 40.

in the case of the reamer ; for this reason great care should be exercised to maintain the tap's lip form when resharpening, for if this cutting-rake is inadvertently reduced, the tap's free-cutting properties will be impaired.

The more usual treatment required is, perhaps, the restoration of a broken tap to render it serviceable for use as a short length tap, intermediate between the taper and plug forms. The end of the broken tap should, in the first place, be evenly rounded off against the periphery of the grinding wheel ; relief is then given to the cutting edges at the tip, as depicted in Fig. 41, by free-hand grinding of the threads behind the cutting edges, and then extending these ground surfaces to form the required degree of taper at the tip. Great care must be taken when grinding one lip to avoid damaging the cutting edge of the following lip.

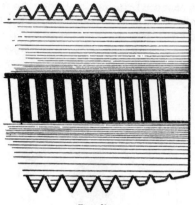

Fig. 41.

Scrapers. There are three forms of hand scrapers in common use, as illustrated in Figs. 42, 43 and 44.

The scraper shown in Fig. 42 is used for working on flat surfaces, and can readily be made from a discarded file, preferably of fine cut to lessen the amount of grinding required to obliterate the teeth ; moreover, it will be found that a fine file will not abrade the skin of the hand when the tool is grasped during scraping operations.

The cutting edge of the scraper is formed by grinding the end of the file to a wedge shape, as shown in Fig. 42B, and, as in Fig. 42c, the end-face is made slightly curved to prevent its sharp corners from digging into and marring the surface of the work.

The object of grinding the sides of the tool in the way shown is to make the tip hollow-ground, and thus lessen the subsequent work required on the oilstone to complete the sharpening.

Great care must be taken when grinding the scraper to prevent overheating of the steel as this would ruin the tool's cutting properties. When the grinding operation has been completed in the way illustrated, the cutting edges are finally sharpened on the oilstone in accordance with the diagrams in Figs. 42D and 42E. As will be seen in Fig. 42D, the sides of the scraper are honed by working the tool backwards and forwards along the oilstone, and, at the same time, the handle is slightly raised in order to confine the stoning to an area near the tip, as in the case

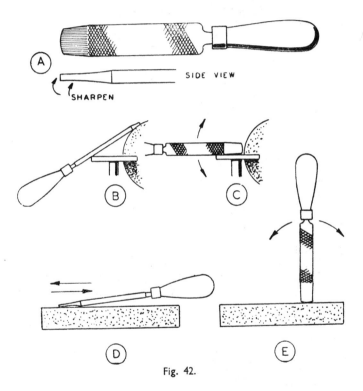

Fig. 42.

of a wood chisel. The end face is then finished, in accordance with Fig. 42E, by working the tool, while held in the vertical position, to and fro along the stone and, meanwhile, imparting a slight rocking motion to form the curved face of the tip.

After stoning, the scraper should be tried on a piece of steel or cast iron, and if it does not cut freely the stoning must be continued until satisfactory cutting is obtained with but little pressure applied to the tool.

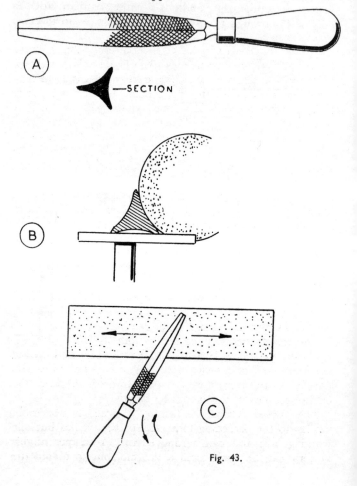

Fig. 43.

When the tip becomes unduly thinned, as a result of resharpening, the tool should be reground to restore the cutting edge to its original form.

The scrapers illustrated in Figs. 43 and 44 are both made for tooling hollow surfaces such as bearing brasses.

The triangular form depicted in Fig. 43 can be made from a triangular file by hollow-grinding its three surfaces against the periphery of the grinding wheel as illustrated in Fig. 43B.

Although the writers have, without difficulty, ground triangular scrapers in this way to form three sharp edges, care must be taken to prevent the file from tilting and its upper edge digging into the surface of the wheel, thus possibly causing serious damage. As an ordinary measure of safety, the file, before being ground, should be fitted with a wooden handle to afford a secure hand-hold. During the grinding operation the file must be kept firmly pressed against the grinding rest but in light contact only with the wheel, and grinding should be stopped a little before the ground area reaches the edges of the file ; in addition, the rest should be set close to the wheel in order to give the maximum of support to the tool.

Those who have misgivings as to their ability to use this method with safety should remove the grinding rest and grind the file free-hand, or, as an alternative, the wheel may be made to revolve in the reverse direction by crossing the belt, but in this case, a lock-nut should be fitted to secure the spindle clamp nut, and thus prevent the grinding wheel from working loose on its seating.

The final sharpening is carried out as shown in Fig. 43c with the blade laid flat on the oilstone, and during the backward and forward strokes along the stone, the handle is alternately raised and lowered to form the curvature towards the end of the blade.

The curved scraper, shown in Fig. 44, is essentially similar to the preceding form, except that it has but one working face and two cutting edges. A scraper of this pattern can be made from a flat file, but to obtain the necessary curvature at the end of the blade the file must be heated to a cherry red and hammered over a lead block, after which, it can be filed to shape and then hardened, and afterwards tempered to a light straw colour. The working face should be ground hollow as in the previous type, and the edges are ground against the periphery of the wheel, as illustrated in Fig. 44B.

The working face is sharpened on the oilstone in the

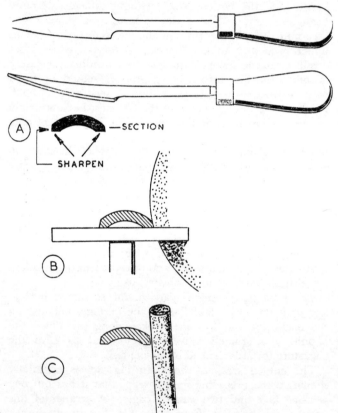

Fig. 44.

ABOVE: A box-mounting for the oilstone of the type advocated by the author. Some workers have suggested that a piece of felt set on the top of the box helps to protect the surface of the stone when not in use; additionally, if well soaked with oil the felt provides sufficient lubricant to fit the Arkansas stone for immediate use. See page 2.

BELOW: The jig detailed in Figs 11 and 12.

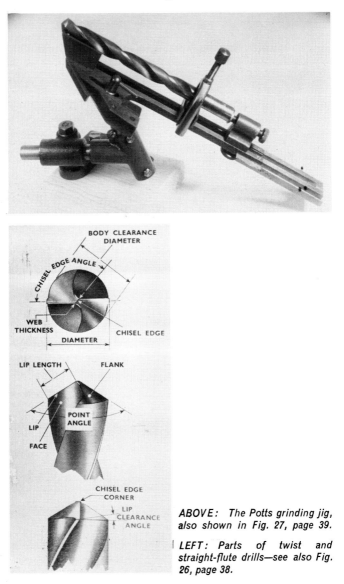

Labels in diagram: BODY CLEARANCE DIAMETER, CHISEL EDGE ANGLE, WEB THICKNESS, DIAMETER, CHISEL EDGE, LIP LENGTH, FLANK, POINT ANGLE, LIP, FACE, CHISEL EDGE CORNER, LIP CLEARANCE ANGLE

ABOVE: The Potts grinding jig, also shown in Fig. 27, page 39.

LEFT: Parts of twist and straight-flute drills—see also Fig. 26, page 38.

A second alternative to Fig. 39 is to make use of an internal grinding attachment having first set the die to be sharpened in the self-centring chuck.   The lathe headstock should be provided with some means of indexing the work in order to simplify setting the die when grinding each cutting edge in turn.

If the work table of the grinding machine will allow, triangular scrapers made from old files can be mounted in a small toolmaker's vice for presentation to the wheel.   In this way the scraper will be held securely and the resulting grinding will be uniform.   The set-up is depicted here. Note that the facet of the file to be ground abuts against the standing jaw of the vice.

ABOVE: The jig that has already been illustrated in **Fig. 12** can be used for dressing the end surface of a hand scraper. The set-up is depicted here. As will be seen packing needs to be placed under the oilstone in order to bring it up to a working height. This can well take the form of a piece of wood planed smooth to ease the movement of the oilstone over its surface. There is little difficulty in maintaining the necessary slight curvature on the scraper's end surface; practice in using the jig will quickly overcome any initial difficulty.

BELOW: A suitable rest for the centre punch that can be attached to the grinder when clipped to the work rest. The fact that the rest is attached to a tilting table has some advantage, as it enables the user to present the centre punch to the grinding wheel with perhaps a little more comfort than would otherwise be the case. See also page 64.

The illustration depicts the method and the correct way to lay the screwdriver against the rim of the grinding wheel itself (see page 62).

It is always a somewhat troublesome matter to ensure that the screwdriver blade is ground evenly. Some help in this direction can be given by painting a ring around the shank of the tool in the manner seen in the illustration. The ring can then be used as an indicator when related to the edge of the grinding rest. In this way uniform positioning of the blade, if not assured, can be much assisted.

Some years ago the author produced a simple jig for grinding screwdrivers. This could be used either for hollow grinding the blade or for dressing it on its flat surfaces. The device comprises a block to hold the screwdriver blade and a rail upon which the block can rest during the grinding operation. The rail forms part of a base that can be attached to the tool rest on the grinding machine when needed. In order to ensure accurate and even grinding the block is provided with a V-groove on each side which rests in turn against the rail whilst the blade is tilted against the rim of the wheel. The principle is depicted in the first drawing.

The device as a whole is illustrated in the second drawing. As will be seen the equipment comprises a table that can be attached to the tool rest and secured by the two fixing screws seen in the illustration.

An adjustable angular fence is mounted on the table where it may be locked by the finger nut seen below the right-hand side of the table.

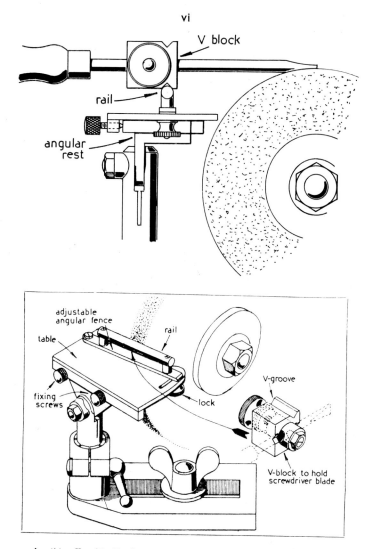

A rail is affixed to the fence; this is used to locate the V-block in which the screwdriver blade is mounted. The block is provided with means for holding the blade which may be turned in this clamping device to suit the form of grinding to be undertaken.

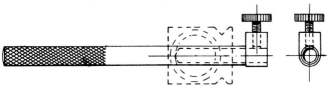

In order to ensure that the blade will be ground evenly two V-grooves are machined in the block immediately opposite one another. In this way each facet of the screwdriver blade is presented uniformly to the wheel in turn thus making sure that the edge of the blade is of even cross section.

When small blades, such as those fitted to watchmaker's screwdrivers have to be ground they must be mounted in a holder in order to complete the work satisfactorily. A suitable holder is illustrated in the final diagram.

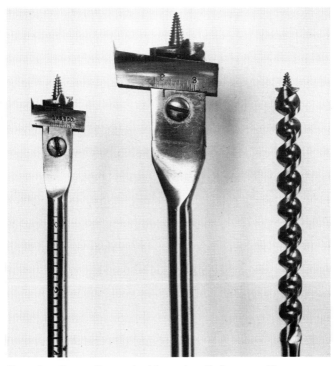

Examples of expanding centre-bits as described on page 93.

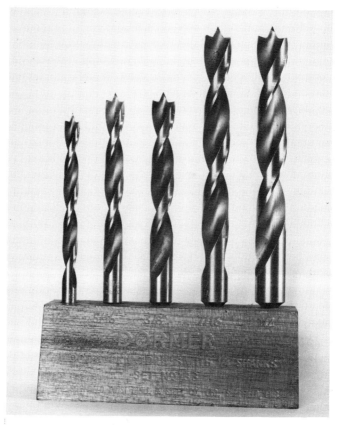

For those who need to use a drilling machine, or an electric hand drill, for woodworking purposes it is possible to obtain special twist drills for use in item. Here is a set of these tools made by Dormer Tools Ltd of Sheffield. The drills are obtainable in sizes from $\frac{1}{4}$ in. dia. to $\frac{1}{2}$ in. dia. increasing in size by increments of $\frac{1}{16}$ in. It will be noticed that they have their shanks turned down so that all will fit into a standard $\frac{1}{4}$ in. capacity chuck.

A plain nib is formed at the axis of the drill, and it is this nib that is used to ensure that the drill itself engages correctly any centre provided for it.

These tools cut freely, particularly if run fast; but in order to provide a clean breakthrough, work should always be backed up with a piece of wood.

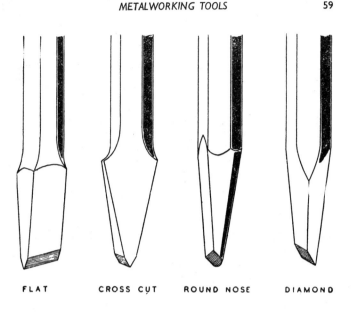

FLAT CROSS CUT ROUND NOSE DIAMOND

Fig. 45.

same way as the triangular scraper, and the sides of the cutting edges are honed with a cylindrical oilstone slip, or with a gouge slip, as depicted in Fig. 44c.

COLD CHISELS. The four common forms of cold chisels in common use are illustrated in Fig. 45. The flat chisel is used for cutting sheet-metal and for chipping flat surfaces ; the cross-cut for forming grooves and keyways ; the round-nosed for cutting oilways in bearings, and the diamond-pointed is usually employed for cleaning out the corners of slots and for cutting grooves.

Although cold chisels are generally sharpened on the grinding wheel, when the edge is but little blunted it can readily be restored on a coarse emery bench stone.

After much resharpening, the tip becomes unduly thick, and reforging is then required to form the tool to its

E

original shape ; this is followed by rehardening and tempering to a dark straw colour, before regrinding the cutting edge.

The correct included angle to which the tip should be formed varies with the type of metal to be cut, but the following table will serve as a guide :

		deg.
Copper and Brass	...	40
Wrought Iron ...	...	50
Cast Iron ...	...	60
Cast Steel ...	...	70

While on the subject of the maintenance of cold chisels, it should be noted that attention to the upper end of the tool is also periodically required, for when heavy work is undertaken the hammer blows will cause upsetting and splitting of this part of the chisel with the result that these jagged edges may cause damage to the hand, and particles of detached metal may endanger the eyes. The head of the chisel should, therefore, be ground from time to time to maintain a smooth surface.

SCREWDRIVERS. Generally speaking, commercial screw-drivers have the tip of the blade formed to the shape shown in Fig. 46, and although this wedge form has the advantage

WEDGE SHAPED, SCREWDRIVER
LIABLE TO SLIP

Fig. 46.

that it will engage in the slots of screws of widely varying size, it has also the disadvantage that, when turning pressure is applied, it tends to rise in the screw slot and lose its grip, unless, at the same time, the axial pressure is greatly increased.

To overcome this failing, the end of the blade should be made parallel, either by filing the tip as shown in Fig. 47A, or by hollow-grinding it as in Fig. 47B.

As the former method greatly weakens the blade, it should be employed only when light turning movements are required ; the latter form of blade, however, fully maintains the strength of the tip, and should be used for

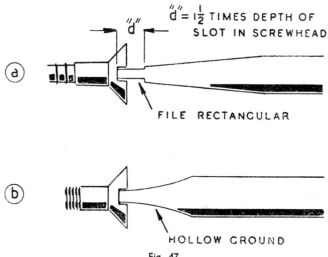

Fig. 47.

all work where it is important that the screw heads should not be marred, as a result of the blade slipping and damaging the screw slot.

If good quality watchmaker's screwdrivers and those used by instrument makers are examined, they will be found to be hollow-ground, for in these crafts the heads of screws are usually highly finished, and any damage caused by an ill-fitting screwdriver becomes all too apparent.

Hollow-grinding is carried out by bringing the blade, when held at a suitable angle, into contact with the peri-

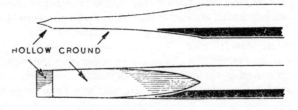

HOLLOW GROUND

Fig. 48.

phery of a small grinding wheel, in a similar manner to that illustrated for grinding the end of a flat scraper. When grinding the blade, great care must be taken not to overheat the steel and draw its temper.

The screwdriver used in the gunmaking trade is of a special form adapted for turning the particular type of screws usually fitted. In best quality guns these screws are very accurately fitted and the heads are hand engraved. Moreover, for the sake of appearance, the slots are so narrow that a screwdriver with a parallel tip would be much too weak to turn them, in view of the fact that during assembly the screws are tightened until they " crack."

The gunsmith's screwdriver, therefore, has a tip of the

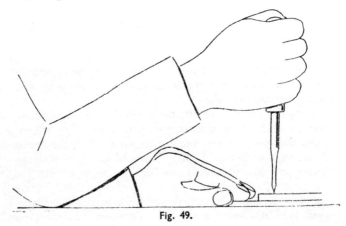

Fig. 49.

form shown in Fig. 48, with hollow-ground flanks meeting at a sharp edge. Needless to say, that if used in the ordinary way, this tool would have but little turning power and would readily rise out of the screw slot. The gunsmith therefore, operates the screwdriver in the manner illustrated in Fig. 49, which allows great downward pressure to be maintained while the full force of the forearm is used for the turning movement.

CENTRE PUNCHES. When sharpening centre punches, it should be borne in mind that the point has to be ground to approximately the correct angle to suit the work, and,

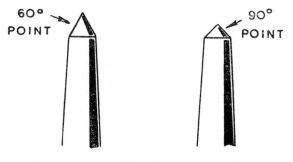

Fig. 50

at the same time, it must be formed centrally. When used for marking-out, the punch should have a fine point of some 60 deg. included angle ; this may be followed, when locating drilling centres, by a punch, as illustrated in Fig. 50, with a 90 deg. point to afford an adequate bearing for the drill-point at starting.

Free-hand grinding of the point is the normal practice, and this will be greatly facilitated by using a support attached to the grinding rest, as depicted in Fig. 51. The V notch serves to locate the punch whilst it is rotated by the fingers against the surface of the grinding wheel.

When a general purpose grinding wheel is used in this way, the abrasion of the fine punch-point will be very rapid, and its surface will be left rather rough. To obviate

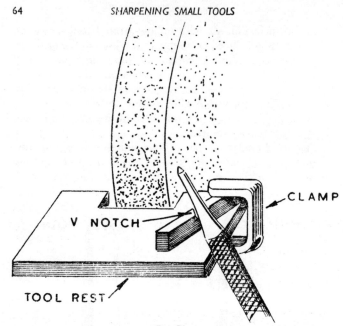

CLAMP

V NOTCH

TOOL REST

Fig. 51.

this, a special grinding machine may be employed for the finish grinding of this and other small tools. A machine suitable for this work, comprising an electric fan-motor fitted with a small India wheel, was described in Chapter II.

SCRIBERS. If a scriber is to operate effectively and mark a clean-cut fine line, its point must be really sharp ; moreover, if heavy downward pressure has to be applied to make the scriber cut, it is quite possible that the guide rule will be displaced and a faulty marking will result.

As will be seen in the drawing in Fig. 52, the blade of the scriber tapers gradually throughout its length, and this taper culminates in an acute-angled working point.

If the point requires to be ground, this is carried out in a manner similar to that described in the case of the centre punch, but, owing to the small mass of metal present, additional care must be exercised to prevent overheating of the steel and too rapid abrasion of the tip.

For these reasons, it is better to do any grinding necessary on a fine India wheel, as has already been described in the case of the centre punch.

Light sharpening of the point is best carried out on a hard oilstone such as an Arkansas.

DIVIDERS. These tools, which are used for scribing circles and marking-off dimensions set from a rule, are easily sharpened, but it is better to give them periodic attention rather than to allow the points to become really blunt.

Except in the event of accidental damage, grinding of the points should be unnecessary, and all that is required to produce a fine sharp point is to rub the sides of the tip with a oilstone slip, as indicated in Fig. 53 ; examination with a magnifying glass will show the progress of the work and will reveal any irregularities of the point requiring attention.

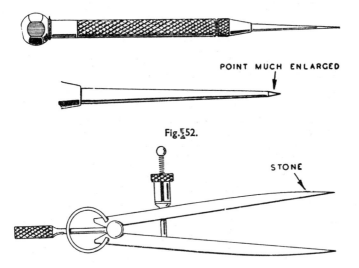

POINT MUCH ENLARGED

Fig. 52.

STONE

Fig. 53.

Both points should be sharpened, for although the centre leg is usually located by a punch mark, it may be required to mark dimensions when stepping-off points along a line.

SHEARS.   The end portion of a pair of shears, as used by the tinsmith and sheet-metal worker, is depicted in Fig. 54, whilst reference to Fig. 55, showing the assembled blades in section, will make clear the cutting and shearing action of these members.

As the handles are closed, the line of contact between the cutting edges travels from the base of the blades towards their tips, and this close contact is maintained by giving a slight curvature lengthwise to one of the blades, also by providing a well-fitting pivot joint.

It will be apparent that, with continued use, wear will take place on both the flat shear-face and on the inclined cutting-face of the blades.   To resharpen the blades, therefore, each is in turn ground on both these faces, but before grinding, the blades should be separated by removal of the pivot-bolt or joint rivet.

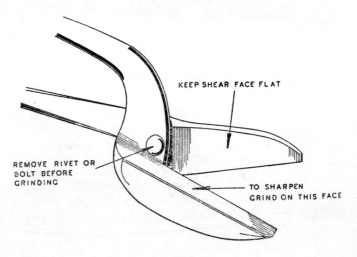

KEEP SHEAR FACE FLAT

REMOVE RIVET OR BOLT BEFORE GRINDING

TO SHARPEN GRIND ON THIS FACE

Fig. 54.

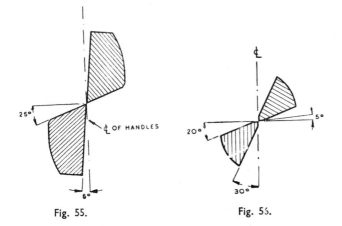

Fig. 55.   Fig. 56.

The shear-face should be ground on the side of the wheel until a flat surface is formed, nearly reaching the cutting edge ; the cutting face is then ground on the periphery of the wheel, until this surface meets the shear-face at a sharp edge.

When the cutting edges have been correctly formed in this way, the blades should be reassembled ; and if a rivet was fitted in the first place, a bolt should be substituted in order to allow of ready adjustment of the blade contact, and also to facilitate dismantling on future occasions.

It should be emphasised that the contact between the blades should not be unduly heavy, for this will cause unnecessary wear of the shear faces. The pivot joint should be well oiled as it is under considerable stress when the shears are in operation.

As illustrated in Fig. 56, shears designed for cutting on a curved path have a narrow and heavily relieved shear face, so as to allow the work to be turned between the jaws.

The grinding of both these shear and cutting faces is carried out as in the case of the straight shears, but great care should be taken to preserve the original angles ground on the jaws, in order to restore the full cutting efficiency of the shears.

END CUTTERS. As these tools are usually made with a riveted joint which is not readily detachable, they may have to be resharpened while in the assembled state.

The design of the bevelled cutting edges is shown in Fig. 57 and 59 and the method usually employed for grinding them is illustrated in Fig. 58.

Care must be taken during the grinding operation to ensure that the cutting edges are made to meet evenly as represented in Fig. 59. There are, however, some makes of end cutters, notably those manufactured by Messrs.

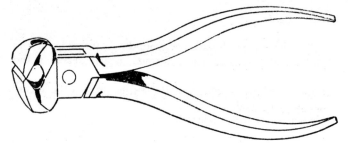

Fig. 57.

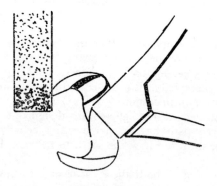

Fig. 58.

RIGHT WRONG

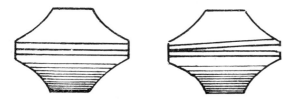

Fig. 59.

Starrett, that have detachable cutting blades which can readily be removed and resharpened in the ordinary way on the grinding wheel and oilstone.

WAD PUNCHES. As these tools are generally used for cutting leather or other soft materials, they can hardly be classed as metalworking tools, nevertheless, they are often required in the workshop for making washers of sheet-lead or red fibre for use during the assembly of machined components.

If the cutting edge of the tool is only slightly dull, its sharpness can be restored by the careful application of an oilstone slip, but where the edge is damaged it will probably be necessary to remachine it to an angle of 45 deg. by a turning operation in the lathe, as illustrated in Figs. 60 and 61.

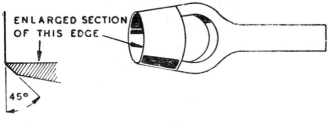

Fig. 60.

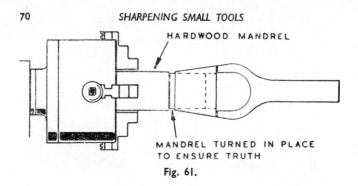

HARDWOOD MANDREL

MANDREL TURNED IN PLACE
TO ENSURE TRUTH

Fig. 61.

To mount the punch in the lathe, a piece of hard wood held in the chuck is turned to fit the bore, and the punch is then pressed firmly into place. If the bore of the punch is much relieved behind the cutting edge, it will be necessary to expand the wooden mandrel to ensure firm holding. This is done by drilling a hole axially in the mandrel and fitting into it a tapered plug, which engages the stirrup of the punch, and so expands the mandrel as the punch is pressed into place.

The mandrel will expand more readily if radial slits are sawn across its end.

Should the edge of the punch be found too hard to be machined with an ordinary lathe tool, a tungsten carbide tool will be effective even if the punch has been fully hardened.

An alternative method of mounting the punch in the lathe is to secure the end of the square shank in the four-jaw chuck, and to support the cutting end with a guide-piece of hard wood, or brass, held in the tailstock. Punches with cylindrical shanks can, of course, be centred in the four-jaw chuck and the cutting edge then machined and honed to a fine finish.

CHAPTER IV

SHARPENING WOODWORKING TOOLS

GENERALLY speaking, the sharpening of woodworking tools is carried out in a similar manner to that employed for metalworking tools. The same abrasive materials, in the form of grinding wheels and bench or hand stones, serve for either purpose, whilst grinding and honing appliances are essentially alike in principle. Furthermore, the object aimed at in either case is identical, namely, to produce a sharp cutting edge of the proper angle in the right place.

Planes

THE BLOCK PLANE. Before dealing with the actual sharpening process, it will be advisable to consider the construction of the planes in general use, in order to ensure that the various forms of the cutting irons used are fully understood.

The simplest type of plane is the block plane, illustrated in Fig. 62, where it will be seen that a single cutting iron is used. This blade is so positioned that its flat face is towards the work and the bevelled edge, which is stoned to sharpen the iron, faces in the upward and forward direction. The angle which this bevelled surface makes with the flat of the blade is usually 30 deg.

To adjust the setting of the plane, that is to say the distance the cutting iron protrudes, the tension screw is slightly slackened and the set adjustment lever is moved upwards or downwards, as the case may be ; the linkage

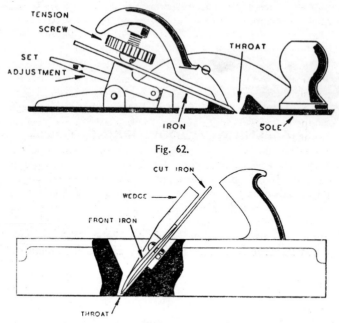

Fig. 62.

Fig. 63.

in this device then causes the carriage, against which the blade rests, to advance towards or to retire from the throat of the plane, carrying the cutting iron with it.

Serrations formed on the face of the carriage and on the under-side of the blade ensure that any movement of the iron does not take place, once the tension screw has been tightened.

Other types of planes furnished with this form of single cutting iron are : the Rabbet, the Fillister, the Dado, and the Grooving plane, as well as all patterns of combination planes used for cutting mouldings and beadings.

THE SMOOTHING PLANE. This plane, together with the jack plane, the shooting plane and the trying plane, has a combination form of iron, as illustrated in the drawing of a jack plane, in Fig. 63, and as it appears when removed from the plane in Figs. 64 and 65. All these planes can be obtained made of either wood or iron, but the type of double blade fitted is similar.

As will be seen in Fig. 64, the edge of the front iron lies a little behind the edge of the cut iron so as to direct the shavings upwards through the throat of the plane.

SHARPENING PLANES. Formerly, plane irons were always sharpened free-hand, and this work was regarded as an essential part of the joiner's or cabinetmaker's craft ; nowadays, however, the difficulties of this operation are often overcome by the use of jigs, which are commendable in that they enable the less expert to obtain good results quickly and with certainty.

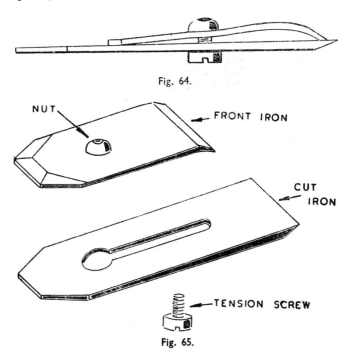

Fig. 64.

NUT

FRONT IRON

CUT IRON

TENSION SCREW

Fig. 65.

When a new plane is purchased it should be carefully checked before use to make sure that the parts have been properly fitted, and, at the same time, the angles of the cutting edges should be measured with a gauge or protractor and their angles noted for future reference.

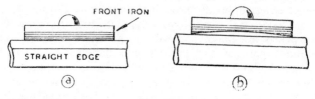

Fig. 66.

As shown in Fig. 66A, the under surface of the front iron must be perfectly flat so that it can bed evenly on the cut iron ; but if this face is found to be slightly curved, as in Fig. 66B, it must be corrected on an emery bench stone in the manner illustrated in Fig. 67. The iron should be moved on a circular path on the stone and with the side of the stone towards the operator ; this will enable the position of the blade to be clearly seen and accurately controlled. If the blade is merely pushed backwards and

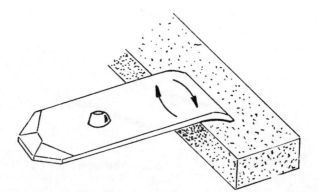

Fig. 67.

forwards along the stone the edge will almost certainly be made rounded.

If the contact face of the front iron is not made truly flat to bed evenly on the cut iron, the wood shavings will wedge themselves between the two irons and will then tend to block the throat of the plane.

Should, however, the curvature of the front iron be found to be excessive and too great for correction on the stone, this must be corrected by grinding on the side of the emery wheel.

Needless to say, the upper surface of the cut iron in both the single and double types of blade must also be perfectly flat, but it is hardly possible that a defect in this particular will be found in a tool of reputable make where correct methods of manufacture are employed ; likewise,

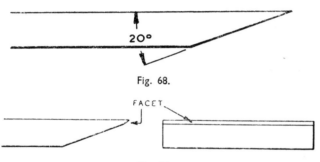

Fig. 68.

Fig. 69.

the cutting edge will be found to lie truly at right angles to the sides of the blade, and the proper angle to suit the work for which the plane is intended will be ground on the cutting edge.

STONING THE CUTTING IRON. As has already been mentioned, the cutting angle of the blade of the block plane is usually 30 deg., but where a double iron is used, as in smoothing and jack planes, this angle is reduced in value to between 20 and 25 deg., and the form of the ground blade becomes as depicted in Fig. 68. During

F

the stoning operation, however, this angle is made more obtuse by some 3 deg. or more, as in Fig. 69 ; this is in order to lessen the amount of work required during the final sharpening on the stone.

To ensure that this angle is accurately maintained right across the edge, a simple stoning jig of the type illustrated in Fig. 7, Chapter II should be employed.

This particular jig was brought to the writers' notice many years ago by a skilled cabinetmaker, who with the aid of this appliance sharpened his plane irons with truly remarkable speed and precision.

As will be seen in the drawing, this device comprises a frame and a clamp to hold and position the blade, and at the extremities of the side-members a hard wood roller is fitted which rolls on the surface of the stone.

The method of setting and adjusting the blade in the jig is also described and illustrated in Chapter II.

Alternatively, the blade can be set on a stone with a dry surface by adjusting the iron until the trailing part of the cutting edge is just clear of the stone's surface, as represented diagrammatically in Fig. 70.

When the blade has been set in the jig, it is moved backwards and forwards along the stone, which at the

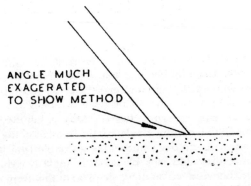

ANGLE MUCH
EXAGERATED
TO SHOW METHOD

Fig. 70.

outset may be a fine grade of carborundum or India stone to give more rapid cutting. To begin with, firm pressure should be applied, but as the work nears completion the pressure should be reduced.

After a few passes have been made, the cutting edge should be examined to see if a wire edge has been formed, as indicated in Fig. 71 ; this can be felt with the finger

Fig. 71.

on the back of the blade, or it can readily be seen with the aid of a magnifying glass.

To remove the wire edge, the blade, while still held in the jig, is applied to the stone in the manner described for truing the front iron and as shown in Fig. 72 ; but it

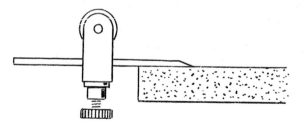

Fig. 72.

is essential that the blade is kept flat to the stone's surface and well-controlled circular strokes used. The two faces of the blade may have to be dealt with several times in this way before the wire edge is finally obliterated.

After the old oil and abrasive have been carefully cleaned from the blade, the final sharpening is carried out in a similar manner on an Arkansas or other stone of hard texture. As before, the blade is reversed after a few strokes have been made and its back is carefully honed to remove any part of the fine edge that has been turned backwards.

Usually, the weight of the jig alone will suffice for the final stage of the stoning, and at the same time, any remnant of the wire edge remaining from the previous honing will quickly disappear, leaving a fine, sharp, smooth cutting edge.

The sharpness of this edge can be tested either against the skin of the ball of the thumb, or on the hairs on the

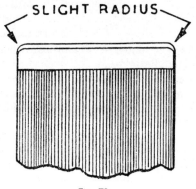

SLIGHT RADIUS

Fig. 73.

back of the wrist ; when the blade under light pressure catches into the skin, or cuts the hairs cleanly, its sharpness is well demonstrated.

It should be noted that the corners of the blade should be formed to a small radius, as illustrated in Fig. 73, in order to prevent the sharp corners from marking the work when the plane is in use. The rounding of the corners is carried out by rocking the roller rest towards either corner at the end of the stroke as the blade is moved along the stone.

The alternative form of commercially-made roller rest, illustrated in Fig 9, Chapter II, has a roller-guide which runs on the bench and not on the stone, but it will be apparent that its greater bulk renders it generally less handy, and rather cumbersome when the back of the blade is honed while the jig is still attached.

GRINDING THE IRON. If the cutting edge of the blade becomes nicked, small notches can be removed on a coarse carborundum stone, but where the damage is greater, regrinding will be necessary. Again, when the original ground bevel has been largely obliterated by honing, the form of the edge should be restored by grinding the blade.

If only a wheel of small diameter is available, the side of the wheel must be used, as, otherwise, the deep hollow-grinding resulting from the use of the periphery of the wheel would seriously weaken the cutting edge.

In any case, when grinding the blade with a carborundum wheel, great care must be taken to avoid overheating and softening the end portion of the iron.

In order to maintain the correct angle and to hold the blade securely, it is essential to employ a simple jig of the type illustrated in Fig. 74. This appliance consists of a wooden block to rest on the grinding table, and a metal strap with clamping screws to hold the blade in place.

It will be appreciated that the angle at the upper surface of the block must be adjusted to conform with the diameter of the grinding wheel, and also with the height of the work above the centre line, as determined by the setting of the rest. The actual sharpening operation is carried out by passing the plane-iron backwards and forwards across the face of the wheel.

THE ROUTER PLANE. As shown in Figs. 75 and 76, this plane has a cutter ground to form a chisel edge at its lower end.

In the example illustrated in the drawings the cutter was made by the writers from a length of square-section tool steel, but those supplied commercially are usually of hexagon form and fit into a groove machined in the tool post.

As the router is generally employed to cut across the

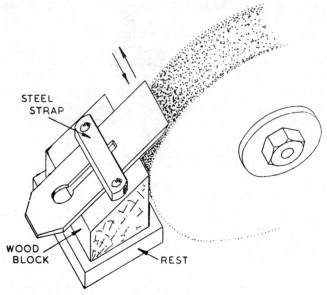

STEEL
STRAP

WOOD
BLOCK

REST

Fig. 74.

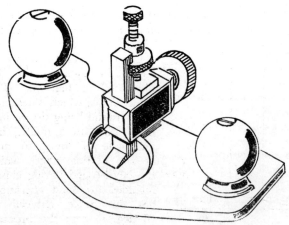

Fig. 75.

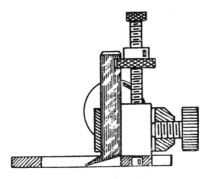

Fig. 76.

grain of the wood, the cutter must be really sharp to give clean cutting.

The cutter should, in the first instance, be ground to the form shown in Fig. 77. The under surface of the sole is then carefully honed on the oilstone to form a regular smooth surface ; the use of the stoning jig illustrated in Fig. 11, Chapter II, will be found greatly to facilitate this operation.

Finally, the upper surface of the cutting edge is honed with an oilstone slip to complete the sharpening of the blade.

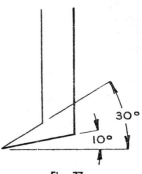

Fig. 77.

CHISELS. Three forms of chisels in common use are illustrated in Fig. 78. The firmer chisel, which is designed to withstand being driven into the work with a mallet, has an angle of some 20 deg. at the cutting edge, whilst the bevel-edged paring chisel, intended for hand operation, has this angle reduced to 16 deg. to ease the pressure required for cutting.

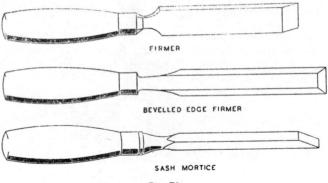

FIRMER

BEVELLED EDGE FIRMER

SASH MORTICE

Fig. 78.

The mortice chisel has a stronger and more obtuse point, as it is subjected to heavy mallet blows, and moreover, leverage may be applied to the handle for clearing the cuttings.

Although all these chisels are usually ground and then sharpened on the oilstone entirely free-hand, better and more consistent results will be obtained by the inexpert, if a jig is used in the way described for sharpening plane irons.

GOUGES. As will be seen in the drawings in Figs. 79 and 80, these tools are hollowed out so that the cutting edge lies on a curve, and for this reason the ordinary pattern of stoning jig cannot be used as a guide when sharpening the tool on the oilstone. The bevelled surface must, therefore, be ground and stoned free-hand, but great care must be taken during these operations to maintain an equal thickness of metal along the whole extent of the cutting edge, for if the bevelled surface is

Fig. 79.

thinned irregularly, an uneven and wavy cutting edge will result.

As the upper hollowed surface cannot be applied to a flat oilstone, a rounded gouge slip is used, as in Fig. 80, to remove any burring of this surface formed during the stoning of the bevelled edge.

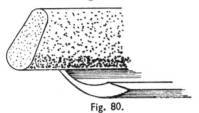

Fig. 80.

SPOKESHAVES. The original form of spokeshave, illustrated in Fig. 81, has a wooden stock, which carries a forged blade, sharpened at its leading edge, and retained in place by the two integral metal tongues shown in the drawing.

Sharpening is usually carried out by honing the underside of the blade on a carborundum stone, followed by finishing the surface on an oilstone; the upper surface of the iron is then honed with an oilstone slip to complete the sharpening of the cutting edge.

Nowdays, spokeshaves of the all-metal type are more generally used, and the adjustable blade, similar to a shortened plane-iron in appearance, is sharpened in the manner already described for honing the blade of a block plane.

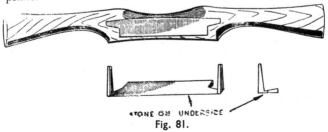

STONE ON UNDERSIDE

Fig. 81.

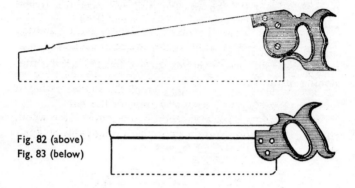

Fig. 82 (above)
Fig. 83 (below)

SAWS.   Two forms of saw are commonly used in the general workshop, the first with a flexible blade shown in Fig. 82, and the second, the tenon saw, fitted with a rigid metal back-strip as depicted in Fig. 83.

The flexible saw is made in two patterns : the rip-saw for cutting along the grain of the wood, and the cross-cut saw for sawing across the grain.

The essential difference between these two forms, the rip-saw and the cross-cut saw, is the design of the teeth. The teeth of the tenon saw are also of the cross-cut form, but are adapted for fine work.

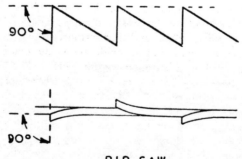

RIP SAW
Fig. 84.

The teeth of the rip-saw are illustrated in Fig. 84, and it will be seen that the front faces of the cutting teeth stand at right angles to the edge of the saw blade, and the cutting edges are formed at right angles across the blade.

In addition, the teeth are set or bent outwards alternately to either side ; this enables the saw to cut a groove or kerf wider than the remainder of the blade so that it can work freely and without binding in the cut.

If a rip-saw is used to cut across the grain of the wood, it will tear the fibres and thus produce a rough and irregular cut.

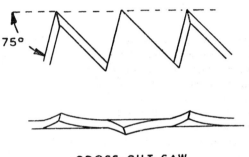

CROSS–CUT SAW
& TENON SAW
Fig. 85.

As will be seen in Fig. 85, the teeth of the cross-cut flexible saw and the tenon-saw form an angle of 75 deg. with the saw's edge, and furthermore, these teeth are sharpened alternately at an angle across the blade so that each presents a chisel-edge to the work. The result of this is that these two lines of chisel edges, formed by setting the teeth, sever the fibres of the wood and cut a clean groove or kerf in the work. The fine, sharp teeth of the tenon saw render it specially suitable for small and accurate work.

SHARPENING SAWS. With continued use, the cutting edges of the saw teeth become blunted, and the set of the teeth is also, in some measure, worn away, with the result tnat additional work is required to operate the saw, and the blade tends to jam in the cut. Moreover, some of the teeth may have become damaged or bent out of line by striking an unseen nail embedded in the wood.

The first procedure is to correct the line of the crests of the damaged or worn teeth, as represented by the upper broken line in Fig. 84.

When the saw has been secured between wooden clams in the vice, a large, flat file is worked along the crests of the teeth until they are again brought into a straight line. This operation will be facilitated if the file is clamped to a wooden guide block as illustrated in Fig. 86.

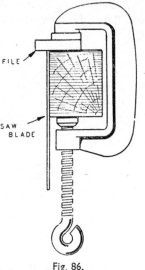

Fig. 86.

After this treatment, the teeth will have to be reshaped, as some at least will be found to be flattened at their points, as shown in Fig. 87.

For this purpose, the saw blade must be held in the vice, but as the depth of the throat of an ordinary 4 in. vice is only about $2\frac{1}{2}$ in., two hard-wood clams some 1 in. thick and 6 in. deep, will be required to give the necessary support to the edge of the saw. In addition, the upper part of the clams should be closed firmly on the saw by means of a G-clamp applied at either end. Alternatively, a special sawmaker's vice with a deep throat can be used for this work.

The teeth are then cut to the correct shape by means of a triangular file, worked at right angles across the blade while held at the exact angle of the existing tooth rear face, as indicated in Fig. 87.

Fig. 87.

SETTING THE TEETH. The next step is to set the teeth, for some of the original set will have been lost either due to wear, or as a result of filing the crests of the teeth. This operation consists in bending the tips of alternate teeth outwards on either side to an angle of some 20 deg., but the amount of the tooth so treated should not, as a rule, exceed one-half of its total depth.

The teeth can be set in this way with a special device, such as the Eclipse saw-set, which is readily adjustable for teeth of either fine or coarse pitch, and at the same time, the setting operation is rendered clearly visible to prevent errors being made. As an alternative method, a hammer may be used to set the teeth against a bevelled block of the form shown in Fig. 88A and B.

This appliance, when held in the vice, locates the saw-edge against a fence consisting of two adjustable screws, so that, after the saw has been placed in position, alternate teeth are beaten down to the bevelled edge with a few light hammer blows.

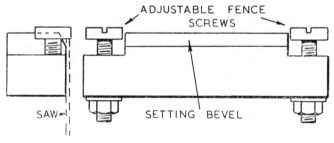

Fig. 88A.

In the case of a saw with fine teeth, it will usually be found more convenient to use a flat-edged brass punch for striking the teeth, whilst, to free both hands for the work, the saw blade is clamped to the extremities of the setting block by means of two G-clamps.

When alternate teeth have been set on one side, the saw is turned over and the operation is repeated on the other side to complete the work.

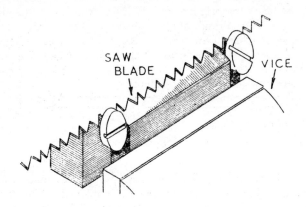

SAW BLADE

VICE

Fig. 88b.

SHARPENING THE TEETH.   After the teeth have been set, the saw is again clamped in the vice by means of the two wooden clams, and the G-clamps are applied to give support to the edge of the saw, which, to allay vibration during filing, should not project more than is necessary.

When sharpening a rip-saw, the front cutting faces of the teeth are cut at right angles, both to the length of the blade and to the line of the teeth, by filing with a triangular file bearing on the bottom of the tooth notch, or gullet, as it is termed.   This should result in the production of sharp teeth of the form shown in Fig. 84.

As is illustrated in Fig. 85, the teeth of the cross-cut saw are usually filed at an angle of 75 deg. to the line of the teeth ; in addition, the teeth are given a chisel edge by inclining the file to form their cutting edges to an angle of some 60 deg. If, however, the saw is used for cutting soft woods, the cutting angle of the teeth may be reduced from 60 deg. to 45 deg.

In order to maintain these angles when filing, a strip of drawing paper, inscribed with the correct angle, may be attached to the wooden clam with drawing pins to act as a guide.

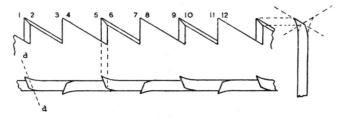

Fig. 89.

Reference to Fig. 89 will, perhaps, help to make clear the details of the method usually employed. The faces 1, 5, 9, are first filed with the triangular file in the direction of the broken line *a*, *a*. The file is then engaged with the faces 2 and 3, until the point of the tooth comes to lie on the line *a*, *a* ; the remaining pairs of faces 6, 7 10, and 11 are then treated similarly. This operation also shapes the faces 3, 7, 11 to their correct form. When the saw is reversed in the vice, the remaining faces 4, 8, 12 are filed to shape in the same way as 2, 6, 10, and the sharpening is thus completed.

CIRCULAR SAWS. The form of the teeth of the circular saw is essentially the same as that found in the hand saw, that is to say they are adapted for cutting either along or across the grain of the wood as in the rip-saw and cross-cut saw, but circular saws with the latter type of teeth are more generally useful as they will cut cleanly either along or across the grain.

In addition to these tooth forms which are found in the smaller saws, saws of larger diameter are often provided with hooked teeth having a more acute cutting angle to promote free-cutting. The teeth of the circular saw are also set, as in the hand saw, to afford clearance behind the teeth as the blade advances into the cut.

SHARPENING. The first operation is to true the tips of the teeth by holding a piece of carborundum or a flat file against the revolving saw.

Small saws can be clamped between two pieces of hard wood in the vice for filing the teeth, but before sharpening, the teeth should be carefully examined to determine exactly the original tooth form and the angles of the cutting edges, in order that these may be preserved when filing.

The actual filing is carried out in accordance with the methods described for sharpening hand saws, but where, as in some saws, the teeth are formed with a rounded gap or gullet, a round or half-round file should be used to form the cutting edges.

SETTING. A mechanical type of saw-set may be used for setting the teeth, but as the teeth lie on a circular path, the flat, bevelled block used for setting hand saws will be found hardly suitable, and, in the case of small

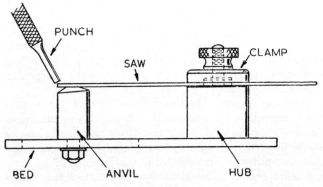

Fig. 90.

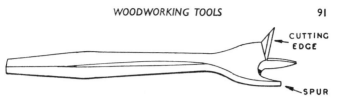

Fig. 91.

saws, the device shown in Fig. 90 is better adapted for the purpose.

This appliance consists of a bed for clamping in the vice, and attached to this base piece is a hub, furnished with a clamp screw for securing the saw, and an anvil with an obliquely inclined chamfer at its upper end.

As will be seen in the drawing, the anvil can be moved radially to engage the teeth, and also rotated axially to alter the angle of the chamfer required for setting them.

After the saw has been secured in place, its teeth are set by striking their tips with a hammer and brass punch to make them conform to the angle of the chamfer set on the anvil.

When the alternate teeth on one side have been dealt with in this way, the saw is reversed for the setting operation to be completed on the remaining teeth.

CENTRE BITS. The centre-bit shown in Fig. 91 is one of the oldest tools used for boring holes in wood.

As a rule, these inexpensive cutters are unhardened and the cutting edges can, therefore, be readily filed when resharpening becomes necessary, or if the cutting edges have been damaged. An edge, sufficiently sharp for most purposes, can be obtained by careful filing with a fine file, or, if preferred, a carborundum or oilstone slip can be used.

The drawings in Fig. 92 show that the cutting edge is sharpened on its bevelled upper surface, and also on its lower face to maintain the necessary cutting clearance.

The spur should be sharpened to a chisel edge by filing on its inner surface only, otherwise the bit will tend to

G

bind in the hole.   The guide point is usually made tri-angular in section with sharpened edges to allow the point to penetrate.

AUGER BITS.   These tools are usually made in the form

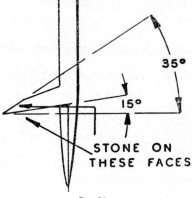

35°

15°

STONE ON
THESE FACES

Fig. 92A.

illustrated in Fig. 93, but there are other varieties in common use of essentially similar design.

The gimlet point with its screw-thread makes the bit

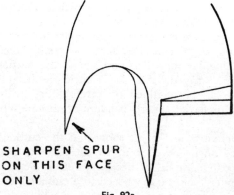

SHARPEN SPUR
ON THIS FACE
ONLY

Fig. 92B.

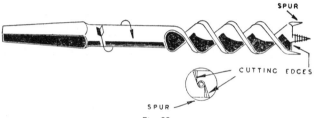

Fig. 93.

self-feeding, whilst the accurate construction of the double spurs and the twin cutting edges, together with the provision of a parallel twist-shaft, renders the tool suitable for the true boring of deep holes.

As the cutting edges of the spurs and also the main cutting edges are not readily accessible, they are best sharpened with a small fine file. The spurs are sharpened

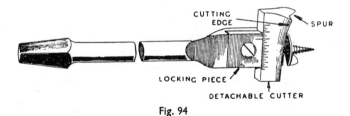

Fig. 94

on their inner surfaces only, for if the peripheral part is reduced in diameter, the bit will bind in the hole.

The bevelled surface above the cutting edges should be carefully filed, and any burrs on the under surface should be removed when sharpening the bit.

EXPANDING CENTRE-BITS. The construction of this tool will be clearly seen in the drawing in Fig. 94. The cutter, which can be removed, or adjusted radially, when the screw holding the locking piece is slackened, forms, in effect, one half of the cutting end of an ordinary auger bit ; that is to say, it has a single spur, and an elongated cutting edge. The base of the cutter is inscribed with graduations to facilitate exact setting. The detachable cutters are highly finished and moderately hardened.

To sharpen the bit, the cutter is removed from its carrier and, as before, only the inner face of the spur is sharpened with an oilstone slip. The under surface of the main cutting edge should also be carefully honed to establish adequate working clearance, but its upper curved surface requires to be stoned with a rounded gouge slip.

SECTION —   —NOSE

Fig. 95.

SPOON AND SHELL BITS. A spoon bit of the pattern commonly used is depicted in Fig. 95, and it will be apparent that, in section, the blade is crescentic in form and has sharp-cutting edges at the tips of the horns,

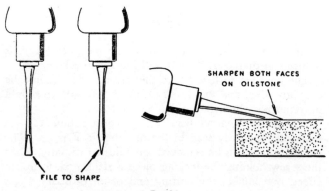

SHARPEN BOTH FACES
ON OILSTONE

FILE TO SHAPE

Fig. 96

whilst a sharp point is provided to enable the bit to penetrate.

The side lips can be sharpened by working a rounded gouge slip in the hollowed portion, and the point is passed backwards and forwards along the surface of the oilstone to form the sharp cutting edges at the tip.

The shell bit is similar in form, except that it tapers sharply from base to tip, in order to enable it to form a taper in a previously bored parallel hole.

The method of sharpening the bit is the same as that used in the case of the spoon bit.

BRADAWLS. As this tool is used to locate and bore holes to receive wood screws, it is essential, for this purpose, that the cutting edge should be really sharp to enable it to cut through the fibres of the wood and not be deflected in so doing.

Although the blade is usually made of tough steel, it is not too hard to be filed when damage to the cutting edge has to be made good. To finish the edge, the bradawl should be sharpened on the oilstone as illustrated in the drawing in Fig. 96.

SCREWDRIVERS AND COUNTERSINKS. Patterns of these tools, suitable for woodworking, have already been dealt with in connection with metalworking tools in Chapter III.

CHAPTER V

SHARPENING KNIVES : SCISSORS : RAZORS : DRAWING INSTRUMENTS

KNIVES. If the blade of an ordinary pocket knife is examined, it will be seen that the form of the blade in section is as depicted in Fig. 97 ; that is to say, the two flat surfaces forming the sides of the blade slope towards each other from the back to near the cutting edge. If these two surfaces were extended until they met, the cutting edge so formed would be too weak to withstand the normal usage for which the knife is intended.

The actual cutting edge is, therefore, thickened and strengthened by grinding or honing two facets, which meet at a more obtuse angle of some 20 deg., and, when sharpening the blade, it is these two narrow surfaces that are applied to the oilstone.

If the blade has become notched, all such blemishes must first be removed by grinding, or by honing on a coarse abrasive stone. When the regularity of the edge has been restored, the sharpening is continued either on an oilstone or on a fine composition stone.

The blade is applied to the stone, as shown in the drawing, with its back raised from the surface, in order to form the required angle at the cutting edge. The blade, with its cutting edge leading, is then moved along the stone, and towards the end of the stroke the haft of the knife is raised, in order to bring the curved tip of the blade into contact with the stone's surface. At the end of the forward stroke, the blade is turned over about its back, and on the return stroke the other side of the blade is similarly treated to form the cutting edge at the correct angle along the whole length of the blade.

If a thin, flexible, feather edge forms at the cutting edge, the back of the blade should be further raised for a few strokes to increase the angle formed at the extreme apex

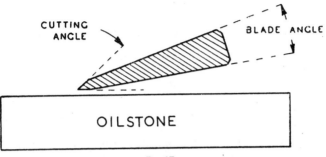

Fig. 97.

of the edge, and, at the same time, the pressure on the stone should be increased. This procedure will break off the feather edge, and the stoning is then continued in the normal manner. As the sharpening process nears completion, the pressure applied to the blade should be reduced.

For cutting leather and similar materials, the slightly rough edge produced by a carborundum stone will be found to give satisfactory results, but where a fine smooth edge is required on a very hard blade, such as a lancet, a hard oilstone of the Arkansas type should be used.

SCISSORS. Scissors are in many respects similar in construction to metal shears, and the method of sharpening them does not greatly differ except in a few important essentials.

In the sectional drawing of the scissor blades shown in Fig. 98, it will be seen that the shear faces are slightly hollow-ground, and that there is a cutting rake of 10 deg. This cutting rake, however, is varied to suit the purpose for which the scissors are made, and it is not unusual in household scissors to find that no cutting rake is given, so that the cutting face then stands at right angles to the shear face.

Furthermore, it will be found that a slight curvature is given to one or both blades in the direction of their length, in order to maintain close contact between the cutting

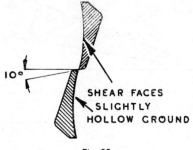

10°

SHEAR FACES
SLIGHTLY
HOLLOW GROUND

Fig. 98.

edges as the shear point moves from the root to the tip of the blades on closing the scissors.

As the scissors become blunted, inspection of the cutting edges will show that they are worn away as illustrated in Fig. 99.

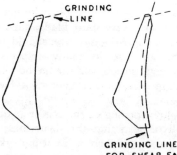

GRINDING
LINE

GRINDING LINE
FOR SHEAR FACE

Fig. 99A.   Fig. 99B.

When, as in Fig. 99A, the wear is only slight, the rounded cutting edge can be restored to its original form by merely grinding the cutting face on the periphery of the wheel, in accordance with the broken line in the figure, but when the wear is more advanced, as illustrated in Fig. 99B, it will be advisable to grind the shear face, in addition to the cutting face, in order to save the removal of an excessive amount of metal.

Although it is possible to grind the cutting faces with the blades assembled, when the shear faces have to be reground the blades should be taken apart by removal of the pivot screw or joint rivet.

The shear face is also ground on the periphery of the wheel, but great care must be taken to ensure that the blades are uniformly ground over their whole surface, otherwise they will not bed together correctly when assembled.

If a fine wheel is used for sharpening the blades, grinding alone may give a satisfactory finish, but should there be any roughness of the edges this should be removed by honing on an oilstone and, at the same time, care must be taken to avoid any rounding of the cutting edges.

When the blades have been correctly sharpened they are reassembled by fitting a new pivot screw or rivet, for the original joint pin will have been made too short as a result of the filing required for its removal.

The jointing of the blades should be adjusted to allow the scissors to work freely, for too tight a joint will cause rapid wear of the shear faces and damage to the cutting edges.

When the joint screw has been properly adjusted it should be lightly riveted over to prevent its turning, but the joint should be tested as the riveting proceeds, and any undue tightness must be relieved by slightly slackening the screw before the final riveting.   Before the scissors are put into use the joint should be lubricated with a little thin oil to prevent unnecessary wear.

RAZORS.   The old-fashioned razor and some patterns

of modern safety razors have blades
of the form shown in section in
Fig. 100. It will be observed that
the flanks are hollow-ground, so
that when the blade rests on a
flat surface, such as a hone, only the
areas at *A* and *B* will make contact
with the surface, and thus only a
small amount of metal will have to
be removed at *B* to sharpen the
cutting edge.

The razor blade is usually formed
so that the thickness of the back in
relation to the width of the blade
gives an included angle of 18 deg.
at the cutting edge, when the blade

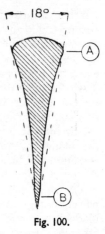

Fig. 100.

is sharpened while lying flat on the hone. Experience
shows that free-cutting, combined with durability, is best
ensured when the cutting edge is formed to an angle of
between 17 and 20 deg.

With continued use and stropping, this edge in time
becomes rounded, as shown in Fig. 101, and the obtuse
angle so formed at the edge greatly reduces its cutting
efficiency, and necessitates re-setting the blade to restore
its cutting properties.

For this purpose, an abrasive stone is used, either of
English, Belgian, or German origin, and the
hone is lubricated with oil or water according
to the type of stone used.

In the case of safety-razor blades of the
pattern illustrated in Fig. 100, a holder will be
required for manipulating the blade at the
correct angle on the stone.

Although the experienced worker can judge
of the state of the cutting edge largely from its
feel on the finger nail, or while being worked
on the hone, this information is usually
more readily obtained by making a careful

Fig. 101

examination of the full length of the blade with a magnifying glass, or low-power miscroscope.

The edge should normally have a slightly waved or rippled contour, due to the scratch marks which result from the use of abrasives, running out at the actual cutting edge.

If notches, resulting from misuse or due to the steel being too brittle, are found they will have to be removed by honing. Moreover, after the razor has been in use for a long time without attention and its cutting properties have become impaired, the obtuse type of edge already mentioned will probably be evident.

The actual honing is carried out by passing the blade, with the cutting edge leading, backwards and forwards along the stone with either a straight or a slightly circular motion.

For the return stroke, the blade is rolled over about its back, and the other face of the cutting edge is then brought carefully into contact with the surface of the stone.

This process is continued until, with the aid of a magnifying glass, it is found that the abrasion marks have all but reached the actual cutting edge. If the honing has to be continued beyond this stage to eliminate notches, or to remove a badly rounded edge, a flexible wire edge may be formed which can be broken off by drawing the blade lightly against a piece of horn or hardwood.

This wire or feather edge is often the result of the blade being too soft, for when the steel is hard, this brittle edge if formed at all, will break off of its own accord as the honing proceeds.

In practice, it has been found that the honing process can be rapidly carried out, under the control of the magnifying glass, if a fine India stone is used in the first place to remove the bulk of the metal. A few passages of the blade will then bring the fresh abrasive marks nearly to the cutting edge, and the time required for the final honing on the razor stone is much reduced.

Should there be any notches in the blade the honing

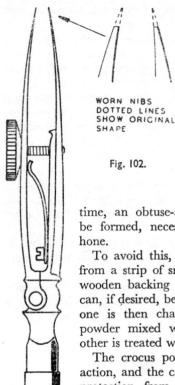

WORN NIBS
DOTTED LINES
SHOW ORIGINAL
SHAPE

Fig. 102.

must, of course, be continued until these are eliminated.

The roughness of the cutting edge, or of the steel immediately behind it, is now removed by stropping to impart the final working finish.

If a piece of very soft leather is used, or if the strop is flexible, the cutting edge will bed into the leather and, in time, an obtuse-angled rounded edge will be formed, necessitating re-setting on the hone.

To avoid this, the strop should be made from a strip of smooth calf skin glued to a wooden backing piece. Two leather strips can, if desired, be mounted on the backing ; one is then charged with a little crocus powder mixed with castor oil, whilst the other is treated with oil alone.

The crocus powder has a mild abrasive action, and the castor oil is added to afford protection from corrosion to the cutting edge after the razor has been in use.

Needless to say, that, when stropping the blade, the cutting edge must follow the line of travel, and the blade must be turned over about its back to make the return stroke.

However well the strop is designed and cared for excessive stropping should be avoided in order to preserve the correct angle of the cutting edge and so postpone re-setting of the blade as long as possible.

DRAWING INSTRUMENTS. After prolonged use, it may be found that, owing to wear of the nibs, drawing pens

Fig. 103.   Fig. 104.

and inking compasses tend to scratch and draw lines of irregular thickness.

This trouble calls for resharpening of the nibs, which, although not a difficult operation, requires care if satisfactory results are to be obtained.

As the nibs of both the drawing pen and the compass are of similar construction, it will suffice to consider the former only.

Fig. 102 shows a greatly enlarged and diagrammatic view of the ordinary drawing-pen nib, which has lost its original form as a result of wear ; the broken lines represent the shape of the nibs in their unworn condition.

If the tips are examined from the side with a magnifying glass, it may be found that a marked flat has been worn as

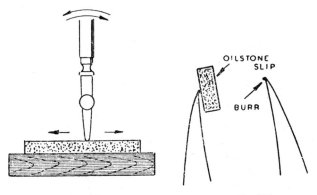

Fig. 105.   Fig. 106.

shown in Fig. 103, where also the thickening of the point due to wear is illustrated.

The correct shape of the nibs is represented in Fig. 104, and it will be seen that the tip should be rounded when viewed from the side, and reduced to a thin edge on its other aspect.

When resharpening the blades is undertaken, the nibs are closed by means of their adjusting screw and the pen, while held in the vertical position, is worked on an Arkansas stone in the manner indicated in Fig. 105 ; the rocking motion imparted to the handle will then produce the curvature at the pen's tip.

The next step is to thin the tips of the blades on their outer surfaces only, by means of an oilstone slip ; meanwhile, the actual edge is kept under observation with the magnifying glass to ensure that the work is carried out evenly.

When the tips of the nibs have thus been sufficiently reduced in thickness, they are separated and their contact surfaces are lightly rubbed with a slip, as shown in Fig. 106, to remove any burrs that may have been formed.

Finally, the nibs are again closed and their points are carefully rubbed with a piece of polished hard steel to give them a burnished finish. It should be borne in mind that, whilst the nibs should be sharp, they should not be so keen as to cut into the surface of the drawing paper ; the final burnishing operation, however, should prevent this.

When the pen has been cleaned with lighter fluid to remove any oil present, it should be tried under working conditions, and if the sharpening has been carefully carried out its performance should be in every way satisfactory.

INDEX

105